SECOND
CORINTHIANS

SECOND CORINTHIANS

by
ROBERT B. HUGHES

MOODY PRESS
CHICAGO

© 1983 by
THE MOODY BIBLE INSTITUTE
OF CHICAGO

Library of Congress Cataloging in Publication Data

Hughes, Robert B., 1946-
  Second Corinthians.

  Bibliography: p
  1. Bible.   N.T.   Corinthians, 2nd—Commentaries.
I. Title.   II. Title: II Corinthians.   III. Title:
2nd Corinthians.
BS2675.3.H83   1983   227'.307   83-13492
ISBN 0-8024-0241-0

4 5 6 7 Printing/EP/Year 87

Printed in the United States of America

CONTENTS

to
David Eldon Hughes
my firstborn, joy, and companion

1

GUIDING CONCEPTS

INTRODUCTION

Flat tires, traffic jams, and dogs that bark at 1:00 A.M. have a way of exposing the depth or shallowness of our spirituality. A reaction of genuine love often seems almost impossible. But the apostle Paul had far more than traffic problems. He was misunderstood and falsely accused. His enemies lied about his desires for money, his qualifications to be an apostle, and his commitment to his friends in Corinth. They even made personal attacks against his appearance. In 2 Corinthians, Paul's reactions to those insults expose a heart of love and deep spiritual insight—truth that can lead us to deeper spiritual responses to life's problems.

Why was Paul able to respond with such maturity? How did he find the right words needed for the very sensitive situation in Corinth? How did he know what to include? What was his process of selection? What emotions directed that process? The answers to those questions uncover the beauties of Paul's heart and teach us how to recognize the world from his point of view—treating people as new creations in Christ (5:16-17). May we see our reactions to life in that light.

HOW TO INTERPRET THE LETTER

The backbone of this commentary is the consistent asking and answering of three basic questions:

WHAT IS THE BASIC CONTENT?
WHAT IS THE SOURCE OF THE CONTENT?
WHY DID PAUL SAY WHAT HE SAID?

Two fundamental beliefs support those questions: (1) Paul had good reasons for everything he said; and (2) his reasons can be found in the needs and problems of the original readers. A look into the lives and times of Paul and the Corinthians is vital for discovering why Paul wrote 2 Corinthians. The why behind a passage also supplies the rationale and direction for present-day application, without which we have truth without reason and arrows without targets.

WHAT IS THE BASIC CONTENT?

An outline of each section of 2 Corinthians shows the *content* Paul presented and the *order* in which he addressed it.[1] Such analysis provides the road map for finding the important link between truth and its application.

WHAT IS THE SOURCE OF THE CONTENT?

What is the source of the content? This question has two aspects: (1) What was the specific source of the readers' needs, questions, or problems? Paul did not waste words; he aimed at specific needs. Therefore, we must always seek to discover the needs that evoked Paul's responses. (2) What resources did Paul use to frame his responses? Were they from his own background, the Christian community, or the Old Testament? Great insights can be gained from the consistent application of these questions.

WHY DID PAUL SAY WHAT HE SAID?

Was Paul's content related to the life setting of the readers, to some problem they had? The point where Paul's resources met the Corinthians' needs becomes the point where God

---

1. Though I have modified his method for the literary form of a letter, I am in special debt to the works of Walter C. Kaiser, especially *Toward an Exegetical Theology* (Grand Rapids: Baker, 1981), pp. 197-210. Special help in interpreting biblical letters will also be found in Gordon D. Fee and Douglas Stuart, *How to Read the Bible for All Its Worth* (Grand Rapids: Zondervan, 1981), pp. 43-71.

meets us today. Their problems are fundamentally our problems, and the way God met them then is the way He speaks to us today.

A PERSONAL NOTE

My goal is to show how God used Paul's knowledge and spiritual reactions to meet some very ugly and deep-rooted problems in Corinth. My prayer is that you will learn some helpful ways to study 2 Corinthians and that you will be led into what only the Spirit can accomplish: personal application and a changed life.

Overview and Key Verses

WHAT IS THE BASIC CONTENT?

A brief overview of 2 Corinthians is the first step in understanding why Paul had to say what he did.

THE CONCERN OVER HIS UPCOMING VISIT

Paul's travel plans pervade the entire letter. The notations of his itinerary expose three aspects of content and order:
(1) Chapters 1-7 relate to Paul's original plans, which he had to change.

> I intended at first to come to you, that you might twice receive a blessing. [1:15]
> But I call God as witness to my soul, that to spare you I came no more to Corinth. [1:23]
> Now when I came to Troas . . . [2:12]
> But taking my leave of them, I went on to Macedonia. [2:13]
> For even when we came into Macedonia . . . [7:5]

(2) Chapters 8-9 speak of the work of Titus among the Corinthians to complete their offering. Paul wanted the matter to be settled before he arrived.

> Consequently we urged Titus that as he had previously made a beginning, so he would also complete in you this gracious work as well. [8:6]

> Lest if any Macedonians come with me and find you un-
> prepared . . . [9:4]

(3) Chapters 10-13 focus on Paul's impending arrival. He hoped for harmony, but would not spare any who persisted in rebellion.

> I ask that when I am present I may not be bold. [10:2]
> Here for this third time I am ready to come to you.
> [12:14]
> For I am afraid that perhaps when I come I may find you
> to be not what I wish and may be found by you to be not
> what you wish. [12:20]
> This is the third time I am coming to you. [13:1]
> If I come again, I will not spare anyone. [13:2]
> For this reason I am writing these things while absent, in
> order that when present I may not use severity. [13:10]

THE REASONS FOR PAUL'S CONCERN

A further probing of this threefold travel structure reveals Paul's rationale behind each section. He wanted them to solve their own problems while he was absent so that when he came they all could enjoy peace and harmony.

Paul's discussion of himself in chapters 1-7 gives his reasons for staying away from Corinth. He wanted to spare them from his severe authority to discipline (1:23). In fact, he remained absent and wrote 2 Corinthians for the same reason; they were still not ready for him to come in peace. The theme of sparing concludes in 13:2, where Paul reasserts that when he came again he would spare no one. Until then, he wants the Corinthians to focus on the things of the heart, not appearance (5:12).

Key Verses: Chapters 1-7

Paul's strategy is to state the *problem* and then provide the *solution*. That strategy is present in each of the letter's three sections. Paul also gives the major *purpose* behind his attempts to correct their problems.

The Problem: You are not restrained by us, but you are restrained in your own affections. [6:12]

The Solution: Therefore if any man is in Christ, he is a new creature; the old things have passed away; behold, new things have come. [5:17]

Therefore, having these promises, beloved, let us cleanse ourselves from all defilement of flesh and spirit, perfecting holiness in the fear of God. [7:1]

The Purpose: We are not again commending ourselves to you but are giving you an occasion to be proud of us, that you may have an answer for those who take pride in appearance, and not in heart. [5:12]

Chapters 1-7 carefully point out the Corinthians' root problem: worldly affections that had closed their hearts toward God and Paul. Paul's solution encourages the readers to make room for him in their hearts (6:13; 7:2). Though Paul claims a great glory for his ministry (chap. 3), the treasure is in earthen vessels (chap. 4). True glory is easily missed if one focuses on the container rather than its contents. That is why Paul only relates to a person's heart realities in Christ (5:12, 16). As Paul drives his point home, he exposes the core of the problem. It is of the heart (6:12) and could only be remedied by "perfecting holiness in the fear of God" (7:1). The entire discussion concerning Paul's ministry in weakness and glory must not be seen as a defensive reaction but as a loving correction.

Key Verses: Chapters 8-9

The Problem: But now finish doing it also; that just as there was the readiness to desire it, so there may be also the completion of it by your ability. [8:11]

The Solution: As it is written, "He who gathered much did not have too much, and he who gathered little had no lack." [8:15]

As it is written, "He scattered abroad, he gave
to the poor, his righteousness abides forever."
[9:9]

The Purpose: I am not speaking this as a command, but as
proving through the earnestness of others the
sincerity of your love also. [8:8]

In chapters 8-9 Paul commends those who would deliver
the collection for the poor in Jerusalem. Charges of greed and
thievery against Paul had blocked the progress of the collection (1:17; 2:17; 4:2; 10:2; 11:7; 12:13-18). Paul tries to correct two problems: (1) the question of equality (8:13-15) and
(2) the question of giving freely from the heart (9:7-9). He
wants the offering to issue from sincere love (8:8).

Key Verses: Chapters 10-13

The Problem: I ask that when I am present I may not be bold
with the confidence with which I propose to be
courageous against some, who regard us as if
we walked according to the flesh. [10:2]

The Solution: And He has said to me, "My Grace is sufficient for you, for power is perfected in
weakness." Most gladly, therefore, I will
rather boast about my weaknesses, that the
power of Christ may dwell in me. [12:9]

The Purpose: All this time you have been thinking that we
are defending ourselves to you. Actually, it is
in the sight of God that we have been speaking
in Christ; and all for your upbuilding, beloved. [12:19]

In this section Paul commends himself as an eminent apostle. However, his boasting in weakness is quite different from
that of his opponents. He corrects their assertion that he
walked in the flesh (10:2). Also, he points out that his free service of ministry should not have branded him as inferior or as
cunningly designed to cheat them. The Corinthians need their
appearance-oriented evaluation of Paul turned around

(12:11). They can only follow the correct pattern of godliness when they understand what makes for a commendable man of God (11:3).

Key Verses for the Letter

The Problem: You are not restrained by us, but you are restrained in your own affections. [6:12]

The Solution: And He has said to me, "My grace is sufficient for you, for power is perfected in weakness." Most gladly, therefore, I will rather boast about my weaknesses, that the power of Christ may dwell in me. [12:9]

BROAD OUTLINE

A TEST PASSED: CONFIDENCE FOR CONTINUED OBEDIENCE 1:1—7:16

A TEST FOR THE SINCERITY OF LOVE: GIVING FROM THE HEART 8:1—9:15

TRUE VS. FOOLISH COMMENDATION: THE REAL SOURCE OF STRENGTH 10:1—13:14

2

LIFE IN CORINTH

PEOPLE AND PLACES: PAUL AND CORINTH

Introduction. What caused the problems Paul faced, and how did he find the solutions? Understanding Paul's past relations with Corinth is the first step toward the answer. The major biblical sources for such understanding are Acts, 1 Corinthians, and 2 Thessalonians. The following material reconstructs the life settings of Paul and the Corinthians. Those settings focus on two problems: money and status.

From Macedonia to Athens. Paul had already forged his philosophy of work and fund-raising when he first set foot into Thessalonica. People had to work for their food (2 Thess. 3:7-10), and Paul used himself as a model of self-support (2 Thess. 3:6-15). This life-style was often criticized, and Paul tackled this criticism head-on in 2 Corinthians. Amid much persecution he left Thessalonica, passed through Berea (Acts 17:10), and entered Athens.

The first visit to Corinth. Paul left Athens and came to Corinth (Acts 18:1) in weakness, fear, and trembling (1 Cor. 2:1-5). True to his ways, he made tents with his new friends Priscilla and Aquila (Acts 18:3). This "work as you go" life-style in Corinth was later thrown back in Paul's face as proof that he was not an authoritative and respectable apostle (1 Cor. 9:6, 15; 2 Cor. 11:7-9; 12:13).

Cities of Paul's Aegean Itinerary

As hostility in Corinth increased, Paul received a special vision from the Lord, telling him not to fear (Acts 18:9-10). Paul mentions his Corinthian troubles in 2 Thessalonians 3:1-3. He was even taken to court by the Jewish leaders of Corinth. The verdict of Gallio[1] the judge was that Christianity was only a squabble within the Jewish religion (Acts

---

1. The date of Gallio's rule places Paul in Corinth around A.D. 50-52. See N. G. L. Hammond and H. H. Scullard, eds., *The Oxford Classical Dictionary,* 2d ed. (Oxford: At the Clarendon, 1970), s.v. "Gallio."

18:12-17). Although that judgment gave Paul freedom under Roman law to continue his ministry it did not insure any bodily protection, as Gallio's "let them be" attitude all too painfully showed (Acts 18:17). The Corinthians had more than ample opportunity to observe Paul's character amid hard and unfair persecutions.

After one-and-a-half years (Acts 18:11) Paul traveled to Ephesus with Priscilla and Aquila (Acts 18:18-19). The couple remained in Ephesus (Acts 18:26) and Paul returned home to Antioch in Syria.

The second visit to Corinth. The second visit of Paul to Corinth is only briefly mentioned in 2 Corinthians 13:2. The brief mention of the second visit masks its great importance for understanding Paul's relations with Corinth.

> I have previously said when present the second time, and though now absent I say in advance to those who have sinned in the past and to all the rest as well, that if I come again, I will not spare anyone, since you are seeking for proof of the Christ who speaks in me, and who is not weak toward you, but mighty in you. [2 Cor. 13:2-3]

That passage contains several facts: (1) the problem was so severe during Paul's second visit that he had to threaten severe discipline; (2) this threat was made with reference to his return, not to his present time with them. The situation was not corrected during his second visit, so Paul discerned that he ought to depart and "in absence" work to solve the problems; and (3) the problem centered on proving that Christ spoke through Paul (13:3). Did he have acceptable credentials? Some were answering no.

There is much debate over whether the second visit to Corinth was before or after the writing of 1 Corinthians.[2] The itinerary followed here concludes that Paul heard about the problems in Corinth when he arrived in Ephesus on his second missionary journey (Acts 19:1—20:1). On his second visit

---

2. For a general survey see Donald Guthrie, *New Testament Introduction,* 3d ed. (Downers Grove, Ill.: Inter-Varsity, 1970), pp. 424-30.

to Corinth (not recorded in Acts), he did what he could to gain a hearing. That attempt failed, and Paul left with an ultimatum: if he returned, he would "not spare anyone" (13:2). Then, soon after his departure, he sent a letter telling the Corinthians to avoid immoral Christians (1 Cor. 5:9), no doubt speaking to the primary issue of the debate during his second visit.[3] Later, Paul wrote 1 Corinthians to clear up some new and some persistent problems. Second Corinthians was written shortly afterwards.[4]

This itinerary is based on several conclusions: (1) 1 Corinthians 16:5-7 represents a *change* of itinerary; (2) 2 Corinthians 1:15-16 was Paul's original plan, and 1 Corinthians 16:5-7 was his "Plan B." On or before his second visit, Paul had spoken of a final double visit (2 Cor. 1:15-16) before he left for Jerusalem. The pain of his second visit caused him to stay away as long as possible, returning only after he had passed through Macedonia (1 Cor. 16:5-7);[5] (3) if 1 Corinthians 16:5-7 is a change from the original double-visit plan, then Paul's statement in 2 Corinthians 1:23, "I came no more to Corinth," meant that he had not been to Corinth since he wrote 1 Corinthians. A visit between 1 and 2 Corinthians is thus excluded. Paul's second visit had to have been made

---

3. Some supporters of the second visit prior to 1 Corinthians are: Philip Edgcumbe Hughes, *Paul's Second Epistle to the Corinthians* (Grand Rapids: Eerdmans, 1962), pp. 31-33 (and p. 52 for additional supporters); R. C. H. Lenski, *Second Epistle to the Corinthians* (Minneapolis: Augsburg, 1937), p. 799 (with somewhat less conviction, p. 14); D. Edmond Hiebert, *An Introduction to the New Testament* (Chicago: Moody, 1977), vol. 2, p. 111 (held tentatively); and Alfred Plummer, *A Critical and Exegetical Commentary on the Second Epistle of St. Paul to the Corinthians* (Edinburgh: T & T Clark, 1915), p. xviii (he states that a second visit prior to 1 Corinthians is a possibility).

4. Hughes, p. 33; Plummer, p. xix; Lenski, p. 799.

5. Hughes, p. 32; Lenski, p. 14; Hiebert, 2:139. For those who hold that Paul originally intended to come to Corinth through Macedonia (1 Cor. 16:5-7) but later changed his plans to the double visit scheme of 2 Cor. 1:15-16, see C. K. Barrett, *A Commentary on the Second Epistle to the Corinthians* (New York: Harper & Row, 1973), p. 7; R. V. G. Tasker, *The Second Epistle of Paul to the Corinthians* (Grand Rapids; Eerdmans, 1958), p. 17; Gordon D. Fee, "KARIS in II Corinthians I. 15: Apostolic Parousia and Paul-Corinth Chronology," *New Testament Studies* 24 (1977-78), pp. 533-34.

prior to the writing of 1 Corinthians. This view of 1 Corinthians 16:5-7 and 2 Corinthians 1:23 produces the following order of events: first visit, second visit, lost letter (1 Cor. 5:9), 1 Corinthians, 2 Corinthians, third visit.

First Corinthians: The life setting in Corinth. An understanding of the life setting of 1 Corinthians is vital to interpreting 2 Corinthians. After Paul's second visit and follow-up letter (mentioned in 1 Cor. 5:9) several things happened in Corinth, causing him to write yet another letter (1 Corinthians). Word had reached Paul through several avenues. Chloe's people reported that the church had split into several factions, each claiming the authority of a well-known figure: Paul, Peter, Apollos, or Christ (1 Cor. 1:12). Such divisions originated in the Corinthians' fleshly and foolish ways (1 Cor. 3:1) and amounted to a division of Christ Himself (1 Cor. 1:13).

Some had become arrogant about Paul's return, which he had promised during his second visit (2 Cor. 13:2). They had misunderstood his letter about immoral associations and thus allowed an immoral brother to fellowship with the Christian community (1 Cor. 5:1-2). Some asserted a superior wisdom, one that surpassed even Paul's (1 Cor. 4:7-10). Evidently, they felt that Paul's words carried little weight (1 Cor. 4:18). Though Paul said he would return with full discipline (2 Cor. 13:2) they were not convinced that he had enough clout for them to worry about. Not all was gloomy, however. The Corinthians were doing generally well (1 Cor. 1:4) and were worthy of some praise (1 Cor. 11:2). From his second visit Paul also had firsthand knowledge of their overall condition.

The Corinthians also sent a letter asking several questions, highlighted by the "now concerning" phrases throughout 1 Corinthians (1 Cor. 7:1, 25; 8:1; 12:1; 16:1). The last question concerned the collection for the poor in Jerusalem (1 Cor. 16:1-4). Titus helped begin this work (2 Cor. 8:6, 10), and the Corinthians were seeking to clarify some details. The picture changes in 2 Corinthians, where we discover that something had caused them to hold back from finishing what they had begun (2 Cor. 8:11).

First Corinthians: The life setting of Paul. Paul wrote 1 Corinthians during his two-year stay in Ephesus (Acts 19:1-2). The visitors from Corinth mentioned above had arrived, as had the questions from the church. Paul had sent Timothy to remind the Corinthians of Paul's ways (1 Cor. 4:17), expecting him to return to Ephesus (1 Cor. 16:10-11). Titus departed for Corinth, probably carrying 1 Corinthians, with orders to meet Paul in Troas.

Titus had been to Corinth within the past year to arrange for the offering (2 Cor. 8:6, 10; 9:2), and the Corinthians were willing to participate. If 1 Corinthians was written in the spring of A.D. 57 and 2 Corinthians in the autumn of the same year,[6] then those mentions of a preparation one year earlier date Titus's work at A.D. 56. During that time, Paul was not only making preparations for the Corinthians' offering but for one in Galatia as well (1 Cor. 16:1). That offering for Paul's countrymen was a high priority for him.

From Ephesus to Macedonia. Paul could not stay away from Corinth forever. He had a mission to Jerusalem, and as spring turned to summer he sent Timothy and Erastus in advance to Macedonia (Acts 19:22). Paul endured much affliction in Asia (1:8) before he departed for Greece to hear the news from Corinth (Acts 20:1). He did not find Titus at Troas, but he went on to Macedonia (2:12-13). Paul finally found Titus somewhere in Macedonia (7:6). He spent much time there giving exhortation (Acts 20:2) and writing 2 Corinthians. He also collected the Macedonians' offering (8:1).

During this period, Paul heard—from Titus and possibly others—the good and bad news from Corinth (10:2, 10; 11:4). Some outsiders had come to Corinth and made the problems worse (2:17—3:1; 11:4). Satan was at work on two fronts,

---

6. Hughes, p. 33; Lenski, p. 14; Hiebert, 2:113, 147; Guthrie, pp. 441-42.

promoting excessive punishment in spite of an offender's repentant attitude (2:11) and using false apostles (11:13-15, 18, 23) to challenge Paul's adequacy (12:14-18). They criticized his weakness in presence and boldness in absence (10:1), favorably classifying themselves as the most eminent apostles (11:1; 12:11).

The problems of "free" ministry and immoral associations had caused Paul enough trouble, but his change of itinerary left him wide open for yet another barrage of criticism, which took him seven chapters of 2 Corinthians to answer. Paul's motives in remaining absent were to "spare" the Corinthians (2 Cor. 1:23), but this change of plans became fuel for his critics. In response, Paul wrote another and final letter (2 Corinthians). Titus and the others who delivered 2 Corinthians were more than mailmen; they were representatives of the churches in caring for the Jerusalem fund (8:23).

The third visit to Corinth. Paul eventually left Macedonia for Corinth (Acts 20:1). With no more waiting or pleading he hoped that, on his arrival, his letter (2 Corinthians) and Titus's ministry would have been effective. He wanted the Corinthians to have a good reputation before the Macedonians (9:4) and to have faith in his credibility before God and men (12:14-18). Discipline was heavy on his mind (12:14, 20-21; 13:1-2).

The details of what happened on Paul's arrival in Corinth are lost in history. We know that he went to Greece for three months, probably the winter of A.D. 58 (Acts 20:3). From there he wrote the letter to the Romans, in which he spoke of boasting in the Lord and working only within his own territory, themes common to 1 and 2 Corinthians (Rom. 15:18-21). He was going to Jerusalem with an offering (Rom. 15:25-26), but he made a last-minute change of sailing plans and returned to Jerusalem through Macedonia. So Macedonia received the double visit (1:15) that Paul had originally promised the Corinthians.

From Corinth to Jerusalem. Paul was accompanied by

Timothy and men from Berea, Thessalonica, Derbe, and Asia (Acts 20:4). The group went on ahead from Corinth and waited for Paul at a favorite meeting place, Troas (Acts 20:5). Paul then hurried along in order to be in Jerusalem at Pentecost (Acts 20:16). During a hurried stop in Asia his last words to the Ephesian elders included disclaimers concerning coveting others' goods and being a freeloader (Acts 20:33-35)—again, common themes in 1 and 2 Corinthians. That must have been a continual criticism leveled against Paul and one against which he executed a consistent and thought-out plan of attack, part of which is seen throughout 2 Corinthians.

Paul delivered the offering to the Jerusalem saints, but Acts does not record the response to the offering. Apparently it did not help Paul in keeping the peace with his countrymen, as Acts 21:20-24 all too painfully show.

PROBLEMS AND SOLUTIONS: PAUL'S MAIN IDEAS

The problems-and-solutions section examines specific words and concepts Paul used in 2 Corinthians to bring God's solutions to the Corinthians' problems.

Authority. What problems would have made Paul speak about his authority in such detail? In 1 Corinthians it was whether or not he had the right to be paid for his services (1 Cor. 9:1, 6, 11-12, 18). But that problem was based on a more fundamental one; was Paul really a qualified apostle (1 Cor. 9:1)? That is exactly the context in which Paul discussed his authority in 2 Corinthians.

The word *authority* is only used in 10:8 and 13:10, which begin and end Paul's reply to slanders against his status as an apostle and his honesty in money matters. Even though those were very insulting accusations, Paul always spoke of authority in the context of positive upbuilding—never for tearing someone down (10:1; 13:10). The section on authority (2 Cor. 10-13) so full of sarcasm and direct attack by Paul, is still couched in the meekness and gentleness of Christ (10:1) for edification (12:19).

Test. If Paul's authority was not adequate, then whose authority was? The Corinthians wanted proof that Christ was in Paul (13:3), and they put him to the test. One test was his life-style. Was he supported by the Corinthians (11:7)? Paul failed that test. Another test was letters of commendation (3:1)—more failure for Paul. Still another was a smooth, trouble-free life (4:7-10). Count Paul out! In the eyes of some, Paul walked according to the flesh (1:17; 10:2) and was full of crafty schemes to get their money (4:2; 12:16).

Paul brought proof for those tests of authority, but not the kind his readers were expecting. He asserted that the true test of authority is given and graded by the Lord, not people (10:18). In that light, he turned the tables and told the Corinthians to test themselves (13:5). His previous letter (1 Corinthians) had put them to a test (2 Cor. 2:9), which they had passed (2 Cor. 7:11, 16). All of this testing, past and present, was not for Paul's own approval but that the Corinthians might do what was right before the Lord (13:7).

Commendation. Since the Corinthians were looking for proof of Paul's adequacy, exactly what commendation did he bring? Second Corinthians has almost a monopoly on Paul's use of the term *commendation*. The last mention of that word is in 12:11: "I should have been commended by you." This is the key to understanding the reason for the heavy emphasis on commendation throughout the letter. The Corinthians *should have* commended Paul. They should have been mature enough to recognize that God was working in Paul and that Satan was at work in his opponents. Because the Corinthians were not able to perceive that, Paul had to labor to show them what makes one truly commendable.

The occurrences of the words *commend* or *commendation* cluster in the first and third sections of the letter (chaps. 1-7 and 10-13). The first mention is by way of a question: "Do we need . . . letters of commendation to you or from you?" (3:1). In 4:2, Paul gave the key to true commendation: "By the manifestation of truth commending ourselves to every man's conscience.'' Conscience, not appearance-oriented status, was the method and target of Paul's commendation. In the last section (10-13), Paul clearly separated his commendation from the ways of his opponents (10:12) by saying that only the one whom the Lord commends is approved (10:18). Commendation is Spirit-effected in the inner person, not affected by grand claims and external life-style.

Boast. If Paul found true commendation through the Spirit, how did the Corinthians prove their authority? They boasted. That one word sums up the Corinthians' whole problem. In 1 Corinthians, boasting centered on factions and opinions about wisdom and foolishness, strength and weakness (1 Cor. 1:29, 31; 3:21; 4:7; 5:6). Boasting also pervades 2 Corinthians. Paul and the Corinthians were each others' basis for boasting in the day of the Lord (1:14, 21). At the end of the first major section, Paul boasted to Titus concerning the Corinthians' repentance (7:4, 14). Between those mentions of boasting stands 5:12, clearly exposing the right and wrong ways of boasting: in heart or in appearance.

In the second major section (chaps. 8-9), money is the main concern. Paul had boasted to the Macedonians that the Corinthians were ready and willing to provide for the Jerusalem offering (8:24; 9:2-3). In the last major section (chaps. 10-13), he divided the concept into three areas: (1) boasting in relation to ones' own work versus boasting in the work of others (10:1, 13, 15-17), (2) boasting in Paul's support-free ministry to the Corinthians (11:10, 12), and (3) boasting in Paul's personal weakness as a means of perfecting divine power (11:16-18, 30; 12:1, 5-6, 9). The subject of Paul's boasting certainly did not go in the direction expected by his critics.

Weakness. Instead of glorying in his strengths, according to the all-too-prevalent norms for Christianity in Corinth, Paul boasted in his weakness. That exposed the Corinthian flaw; an infatuation with a superficial and worldly outlook. Such is clear from Paul's words in 5:12 and 6:14—7:1.

In 1 Corinthians weakness falls into two major groupings: (1) in 1 Corinthians 8-9, those who cannot eat meat sacrificed to idols are called weak (1 Cor. 8:7, 9-12; 9:22); (2) in 1 Corinthians 1-4, Paul distinguishes between the strong and the weak, the wise and the foolish, in order to demonstrate that, though his coming did not conform to worldly standards, he came in the very power of God. He would not void the wisdom of the cross (1 Cor. 1:17).[7] The Corinthians' tendency to factions and arrogance may be closely aligned with the invading group of false apostles addressed in 2 Corinthians. Those invaders would have pandered to the Corinthians' already strong desire for worldliness.

Instead of coming in the power of worldly wisdom, the apostle Paul came "in weakness and in fear and in much trembling" (1 Cor. 2:3). But what sort of weakness is Paul talking about? It is doubtful that it was a result of defeat in Athens (Acts 19:32-34). Paul describes how he came to *any* city. Weakness, fear, and trembling were the mode of his ministry. That desribes how one who is thinking rightly about his relation to God and humanity will operate, in contrast to the cocky and self-reliant wisdom of the world. Paul uses this word-group in 2 Corinthians 7:15, Ephesians 6:5, and Philippians 2:12. Boasting and the strong-vs.-weak debate form the life setting of 2 Corinthians. There were factions operating on the basis of external fleshly wisdom, asserting superiority over Paul, who looked weak by comparison (10:1; 11:21). But more important, Paul stresses his personal and theological experience of weakness.

His personal experience of weakness (11:30; 12:5, 9-10) showed how God's power is "perfected in weakness" (12:9). Paul's personal experience of direct divine revelation detailed this conviction. God's grace was sufficient. The reason? Weakness perfects power. When Paul was weak, then he was

7. H. Chadwick, " 'All Things to All Men' (I Cor. IX 22)," *New Testament Studies* 1 (1954-55): 261-75.

strong. Paul's theological experience of strength in weakness is evident in 13:3-4, 9. Christ was crucified because of weakness, but He lived in the Corinthians in strength. The implications are clear. Until the Corinthians were glorified, they had to count on the strength of the resurrected Christ within them and to cease infatuation with the externals of worldly power.

Comfort. Paul uses the noun and verb often in 1 and 2 Corinthians to refer to exhortation (1 Cor. 1:10; 4:14, 16; 14:3, 31; 16:12, 15; 2 Cor. 8:4, 6, 17; 9:5; 10:1; 12:8, 18). However, in 2 Corinthians 1-2 and 7, Paul uses the noun and verb seventeen times with the specific meaning of "comfort." What caused him to speak so much of comfort? Chapters 1 and 7 focus on comfort from the Corinthians' repentance (2:9, 7:11). Chapter 2 uses comfort with reference to the repentant brother. Forgive the brother (2:8) and forgive me (12:13), cries Paul. Only then would pastor and people share mutual open-hearted comfort (6:13).[8] Comfort issues from the Corinthians' earnestness for Paul and forms the basis for continued ministry of the offering (8-9) and last-minute discipline for those who still needed it (10-13).

SUMMARY

Money and status were the continual problems Paul faced at Corinth. His free ministry was taken to indicate second-rate qualifications and a crafty way to get money by means of his associates. The Corinthians cloaked their status-seeking in the guise of wisdom and maturity but actually opened themselves to immoral relations, a disregard for God's words through Paul, and ultimately a voiding of the reconciling

---

8. They had been exposed to this manner of ministry already, possibly knowing Paul's words (written from Corinth) in 1 Thessalonians 3:5-10, where many of the themes found in 2 Corinthians are present, including comfort, mutuality, joy, and completion.

power of the cross of Christ. Second Corinthians presents a moving example of a spiritual response to difficulties, a fusion of praise and correction.

3

MUTUAL TRUST REAFFIRMED:
A FIRST DEFENSE

(1:1—2:17)

The first lines of a normal first-century letter give the names of the writer and his addressees. Second Corinthians carries the names of Paul and Timothy and is addressed to the church in Corinth and the larger area of Achaia (1:1). The way Paul describes himself ("by the will of God") highlights the problem to which he is speaking and builds the foundation for all that follows. God willed Paul's authority; Paul did not seek it out on his own. That somewhat stock Pauline phrase (1 Cor. 1:1; Eph. 1:1; Col. 1:1; 2 Tim. 1:1) does not diminish its relevance for the Corinthian problems. Paul's authority resulted from God's initiating will. Behind any attack on his person or ministry stood a questioning of the authority of God who had willed his ministry into being. Paul's movement from authority in ministry to God as source of authority explains his digression concerning God's faithfulness in 1:18-22.

Paul describes his readers corporately and personally. The phrase "church of God" shows the identity and ownership of the community and provides the context for Paul's severe, though always edifying, discipline. It was God's community and therefore subject to the absolutes of His compassion (1:3; 10:1) and His holiness (7:1). The personal description "saints" further clarifies the Corinthians' standing before God and the character trait (holiness) necessary for correcting

27

their problems. Paul will later tell these people that they are being taken in by the superficial status of the world (6:14); that they are having problems being generous (8-9); and that they are seriously questioning Paul's relationship to Christ (10:7; 13:3). Yet he is still able to wish all of God's grace and peace on them (1:2). "Grace" is the act of God that would meet their needs. "Peace" is the resultant interpersonal and man-to-God wholeness. Second Corinthians exposes specific points needing the grace of God in order to bring about peace of heart, mind, and community. Peace and grace sound the beginning and ending notes of the letter (1:2; 13:11, 14).

We must never forget Paul's undying love for his people, even when he was in the middle of applying severe discipline. He learned that from his heavenly Father ("our Father," 1:2) and saw it modeled in the Son. The next section shows that the Father and Son are the source of all grace and peace.

MUTUALITY IN SUFFERING AND COMFORT (1:3-11)

Individual enablement (1:3-5). There are three descriptions of God in 1:3-4. He is "the God and Father of our Lord Jesus Christ"; "the Father of mercies and God of all comfort"; and the one "who comforts us in all our affliction." Those three descriptions are the basis of Paul's main point; the result ("so that," 1:4) of having such a comforting God is the ability to share comfort with others. The concept of shared comfort is crucial to understanding Paul's thoughts and motivations throughout the letter. His initial point is that even his sufferings (the weaknesses so despised and criticized by his enemies) were actually a positive force in his ministry. Paul would be accused of selfishness and fleshly fickleness (1:17). From the start he stresses that all he did was not for himself, but for *them*. That explains the rather quick shift of focus from Paul's comfort to that of others.

Jesus the Messiah is central to his process of sharing comfort. In 1:2 we read, "God our Father." In 1:3, God is the "Father of our Lord." Jesus assumes the position of sonship in 1:3, because He is the medium of both comfort and sufferings (1:5). Verse 4 speaks of "our affliction," but 1:5 ("the sufferings of Christ are ours") identifies the true sufferer, Christ. That explains why 1:5 begins with "for"; it defines the reason behind Paul's ability to share comfort with others. If they share in Christ's sufferings they also share in His comfort. Abundant suffering brings abundant comfort.

But Paul is speaking about his own sufferings. How did the sufferings of Christ come into the picture? Christ, as the medium of both suffering and comfort, had always been on Paul's mind. Paul's troubles were incurred as he served the believers in the work of Christ; 1:6 brings that thought out more clearly. Paul did not take his trials personally. Just as the Lord Himself was the object of Paul's persecutions of the church (Acts 9:4, "Why are you persecuting Me?"), so Paul saw his own trials as continued suffering inflicted upon Christ (see John 15:20-21).

The events of Paul's life were not split up into two segments—the good being part of God's will and the bad somewhat apart from His best. Paul saw the good and the bad as all within his life in Christ. But the bad was always swallowed up by the good. As Christ's resurrection swallowed up the agony of His death, so the comfort of His resurrection swallowed up the pain of Paul's suffering. That was what he wanted the Corinthians to understand. Suffering and weakness are not outside our life in Christ; they are the only pathway to experiencing God's strength and comfort.

Mutual fellowship (1:6-7). Verse 6 continues the other-oriented trust of suffering and comfort that Paul began in 1:4. The first part of the verse must be understood in light of 1:5; suffering and comfort come simultaneously from God through Christ. But Paul wants only comfort for the Corinthians. He shares with his children all the comfort he has found in his suffering. The latter half of verse 6 expands the concept of mutuality by giving the key to experiencing Christ's comfort: patience. What is comfort? Paul defines it as the ability to endure trials patiently, not to escape from them. The Greek word for *endure* means to "bear up under" something, not to get out from under it.

Paul had great hope (1:7) that this mutuality of suffering and comfort was active and well-understood between himself and the Corinthians. He counted on their sympathy (7:5-16). To share sufferings is to share comfort. He further develops the sharing idea in 1:8-11; comfort works simultaneously with suffering. That placed the Corinthians on the same level of weakness as Paul. To deny the worth of suffering, as the Corinthians tended to do, was to deny their desire to have full fellowship, not only with Paul but with the risen Lord. This link to the ways of God in Christ underlies Paul's later discussions of adequacy, commendation, and weakness.

Sharing the sufferings (1:8-11). What does the "for" of 1:8 explain? There is something that can block the process of sharing comfort: ignorance. Paul had already spoken in general of affliction (1:4, 6) and sufferings (1:5). Verses 8-11 provide a specific flesh-and-blood example of how suffering can bring about true comfort. Paul mentions his serious trouble: affliction in Asia and despair of life. Specifying troubles ("we do not want you to be unaware," 1:8) is necessary to sharing comfort. Why should the Corinthians be unaware, when it is just such awareness that provides the way to true comfort? One reason is suggested by his opponents' arguments against Paul; to speak of such suffering would be to admit great weakness and therefore to weaken any claims to adequacy. But would the Corinthians be willing to take the suffering along with the comfort? Or would they follow the opponents and try to deny all that smacked of weakness? Paul shows that weakness, when admitted, drives us to trust in God, the One who can even raise the dead (1:9).

Verse 9 begins with a contrast ("indeed" should be replaced with "but"). The contrast is between someone focused on the suffering itself and another who focuses on God's purpose for the sufferer. That is the example of patience in suffering. Paul's point is that comfort and patience in trials come from learning the lesson of 1:9. Even he needed that lesson.

Another description of God follows in 1:10. He "delivered" and "will deliver." That last remark especially needed clarification. How could Paul have known that God would deliver him? Verses 10b-11 explain his confidence. God would deliver him in order that a multitude might give thanks to God (1:11). In saying that, Paul bound the readers more closely to himself. He needed them and their prayers to bring in a harvest of thanksgiving. How could Paul be so sure that the Corinthians would care to labor so vigorously in prayer for him, especially in light of their severe problems? The next section explains, in part, his further confidence.

THE GOOD INTENTIONS FOR THE FIRST ITINERARY (1:12-22)

From this point on the purpose expressed in 5:12 controlled Paul's thoughts and his selection of data as he began his answer to the question of pride in appearance rather than in heart. He supplied internal standards for commendation and adequacy rather than the externals in which his opponents boasted.

Paul's confidence (1:12-14). Paul had confidence in the Corinthians' prayer support (1:11) because he knew his conscience was clean. Human conscience was the proving ground for Paul's adequacy and the target of his arguments: "by the manifestation of truth commending ourselves to every man's conscience in the sight of God" (4:2). That explains the "for" of verse 12. Paul was certain that the Corinthians would pray for him because they knew his behavior and conscience were clean.

That thought returns the reader to Paul's statement in 1:7. He knew they were sharers on the basis of a demonstrable past involvement. "Not in fleshly wisdom" (1:12) shows that Paul was preparing to answer the accusations of 1:17 and 10:2 regarding his change of itinerary. Also, in his most recent let-

ter (1 Corinthians) he had spent much time contrasting the
wisdom of the world with the wisdom of God (2 Cor. 1-4). In
2 Corinthians Paul contrasts fleshly wisdom with holiness and
godly sincerity, themes he would develop extensively.
Holiness is his goal and capstone in chapters 1-7 (7:1), and
sincerity is his way of describing a truly spiritual and adequate
gospel ministry (2:17; 4:2).

Verses 13-14 explain "especially toward you" (1:12). Verse
13 gives one specific example of Paul's good conscience; the
honesty of his letters, which was part of the honesty of his
life. His earlier letters had been criticized (10:9-11), but in
1:13 he refers to what he has written in the previous twelve
verses.

The interpretive key to Paul's whole understanding of
mutuality lies in 1:14, with reference to what the Corinthians
had at least partially understood. That verse presents a world
view that undergirded Paul's entire concept of what bound
him to the Corinthians; when the day of the Lord arrives,
they will be each others' reasons for pride. He hoped they
would fully understand that (1:13). Their future mutual joy
before the Lord had to pervade their present attitudes toward
each other. They were bound together in an eternal calling of
life and redemption in Christ. How could they even think
about being less than open and warm with each other and
with Paul? How could they have split up into arrogant factions and turned a cold heart to the one who labored so
sacrificially to bring them the great message of salvation?

Implications of fickleness (1:15-22). As Paul took up the
matter of the change in his itinerary, he emphasized how
much the Corinthians would have been profited by his visit.
His intentions were always positive and full of confidence.
What is "in this confidence" (1:15)? He had spoken of his
"proud confidence" (1:12) concerning his past behavior
among them. Why should they think that his change of plans
was anything other than his usual best and positive actions?
"At first" (1:15), as presented in an earlier itinerary, Paul

would have visited them twice, which he knew (in his confidence of their good relationship) would be a mutual blessing. But the great troubles in Corinth and his sorrowful visit had put an end to those hopes. Paul had to stay away in order to spare them his severe discipline. But some, interpreting his change as a fleshly vacillation, had questioned his intentions; did Paul stay away because he disliked them?

Paul uses the same word for *intended* four times: once in 1:15 and three times in 1:17 (translated "intended" the first two times and "purpose" the last two times). He shifts from "I" (1:17) to "our" (1:18) to specific names (1:19) as he deals with slanders extending to his whole team.

Verses 18-22 describe tne implications of such slander in relation to God's faithfulness. At first that may not seem immediately relevant. Why did Paul bring God's character into the picture? Because to impugn Paul was to impugn God. Paul identifies his actions with the God of comfort and redemption! He would answer the specific charge regarding his change of plans later (1:23). But first a caution; if the Corinthians believed the criticism about Paul, they would find that they had been critical of God. God's faithfulness (1:18) was the foundation for His work in Christ ("in Him," 1:19-20; "in Christ," 1:21) and His ministry through Paul. Looking at externals, the Corinthians missed God's faithfulness reflected in Paul's ministry.

The gospel proclamation (1:19) could not be yes and no. When one is in Christ there is no playful fickleness on God's part. He freely gives us all of His promises in Christ (1:20). (The key promises for Paul's argument are found in 6:14—7:1.) God confirms the entire sum of divine promises for restoration and forgiveness from Genesis onward in the Christian's life. God never changes the rules after awarding the prize of eternal life in Christ.

The anointing (1:21) and sealing work (1:22) of the Holy Spirit make those promises come to life. The words *Christ* and *anointed* come from the same Greek root. Christ means "the anointed one"; therefore, as the Spirit anointed Christ so Christians share in His anointing. We become "anointed ones" in the redemption found in Christ. God has "sealed us" (1:22), marked us as His permanent property, and given us the realization of belonging to Him by our experience of the Spirit. The Spirit is the "pledge" (1:22). But of what? Of eternal glory at the day of the Lord (1:14). The Spirit is the believer's present and active agent of God in comfort (1:3-6), hope (1:7), and any appropriate pride or confidence (1:12, 14). The critics overlooked this heart-level witness of God (1:22) in their rush to jump on external weakness or change.

How does all of that explain why Paul changed his itinerary (1:15-17)? Why would one change potentially void his entire credibility? Because the Corinthians could recognize neither Christ's sufferings (1:5) nor God's faithfulness and glory manifested in Paul and his companions. The Spirit was God's bond between Paul and the Corinthians and also His confirmation of Paul's divine approval. The charge of fleshly action brought that bond and approval under suspicion. The Corinthians needed to share in God's suffering and comfort (1:3-11) and to affirm His faithfulness in the Spirit (1:21-22). They were to reaffirm God's faithfulness in the gospel *and* in Paul's decision-making process, lest their faith in the gospel fall along with their disillusionment with Paul. The issue was indeed that serious (see 11:3-4).

THE GOOD REASON FOR THE CHANGE (1:23—2:11)

The link to the previous section is mutual joy (1:24) in the day of the Lord (1:14). If joy is to be the future's aim, it must also be the present's reality. That explains Paul's change of plans; he would remain absent as long as possible to ensure mutual joy when present. Because of the highly sensitive situation in Corinth, Paul had to be defensive and careful.

To spare now (1:23). Paul did not return as planned, in order to spare them his promised severe discipline (1 Cor. 4:21; 2 Cor. 13:2). His absence, however, was full of efforts to help them. He had written them two letters (1 Corinthians

and the one mentioned in 1 Cor. 5:9) and had sent Timothy
and Titus to minister to them.

To share joy later (1:24). Though he could exercise harsh
discipline, Paul clarified that he was speaking as a co-worker
for their joy, not as a dictator ("lord it over," 1:24). He was
not their source of judgment or joy, but only one of their
"bond-servants for Jesus' sake" (4:5). But that servant concept, vital for any ministry, becomes filled with potential self-
contradictions when the servant must exercise discipline.
Perhaps to the surprise of his hearers, Paul viewed the situation as an issue of joy, not one of faith. He was not addressing heretics ("in your faith you are standing firm," 1:24); at
stake was the *outworking* of their faith. The ability to
distinguish between issues of faith and fellowship is always
crucial. The dictatorial attitude adopted by the false apostles
(11:20) had no part in Paul's joy-oriented work with the Corinthians.

The reversed situation (2:1-3). After much thought, Paul
("for my own sake," 2:1) came to a firm conclusion ("deter-
mined," 2:1). He would not come again in sorrow. His
disastrous second visit had settled that—not because of personal anger but interpersonal sorrow (2:2). Verses 12-14 are
again vital for appreciating Paul's thrust here. Eternal joy,
not sorrow, should characterize Christian fellowship. The
situation was reversed from what it should have been (2:2).
Paul's great desire for mutual joy (1:24) could not be met in
the middle of fightings and conflicts. He had said this before
(2:3), probably in 1 Corinthians (1 Cor. 4:19-21). He made
every effort, therefore, to help the Corinthians solve their
problems before his return.

The point of 1 Corinthians (2:4). Paul wrote to show love,
not to make a final negative judgment. His harsh exhortation
expresses as much love as his praise and encouragement. Paul
worked for their joy, not their sorrow. The situation in

1 Corinthians caused Paul "much affliction and anguish of heart" (2:4). How could they have joy when the situation was so bad? Paul hoped to clear up the problems, so that they might all have the joy of the Lord. This discussion of sorrow must be read in the light of 7:8-13, where Paul draws the crucial distinction between the sorrow of the world and sorrow according to God.

The sorrow and correction issuing from 1 Corinthians (2:5-11). Even when speaking of a past sorrow, Paul shared two thoughts that contributed to his goal of joy: (1) he presented his sorrow within a community-wide context: "to all of you" (2:5), and (2) he did not want to pour salt on an already healing wound ("in order not to say too much" [2:5]) when referring to the very wide scope of the past offense. He was positive and upbeat. The details of the sin were not to be aired once again. The sinner had caused great sorrow (2:5), had been punished and had experienced sorrow (2:6), and was then in danger of being "overwhelmed by excessive sorrow" (2:7).

The severity of the offense was matched with an equally strong ("sufficient," 2:6) punishment, probably the one Paul ordered in 1 Corinthians 5. The least he had hoped for was the offender's salvation in the day of the Lord (1 Cor. 5:5), but the fellow had fully repented. The offender was then faced with the Corinthians' reticence to match his repentance with their forgiveness and was in danger of being crushed. After all, love was the context of the discipline in the first place (1 Cor. 5:5b). Paul had written the whole of 1 Corinthians so that the Corinthians would know his love (2:4) and that he might know their obedience (2:9). Therefore he commanded ("wherefore," the strongest Greek word to state a conclusion) that they reaffirm love ("your" is not in the Greek, 2:8) for him. Repentance must be met by full restoration in love. The command to reaffirm love represented another step in the display of Paul's love and the Corinthians' obedience.

Paul forgave in the full "presence of Christ" (2:10), a presence that allows no unforgiving hearts and reflects all of the positive aspects of God's forgiveness. Paul stressed mutuality in forgiveness to show that he had no hard feelings about the past offense. Any reticence to forgive was a satanic scheme (2:11), possibly fostered by Satan's ministers (11:14-15). Paul exposed the multifaceted schemes of Satan, leaving the implications up to the Corinthians. They were not ignorant of Satan's schemes, but would they obediently follow the apostle's instructions to combat them?

The case of the repentant offender presents another aspect of Paul's proof that he was for—not against—the Corinthians. The issue of miserly forgiveness was a small illustration of the larger complex of problems between Corinth and the apostle. They were still closed in heart toward the repentant brother and also toward Paul (6:12-13). He had issued stern correctives, and they had responded in obedience. But were they willing to restore themselves to full fellowship with Paul? He could forgive and forget, but could they? Paul hoped they would accept those thoughts as adequate proof of his overall good intentions (as specifically related to the itinerary change). Paul would once more use his journey from Ephesus to Macedonia to show them the marks of true pride in heart rather than appearance.

PAUL'S CONTINUED CONCERN (2:12-17)

The resumption of the itinerary: Troas to Macedonia (2:12-13). Paul's itinerary provided the framework for his correctives to the Corinthians' disdain for weakness and preoccupation with externals.

>ITINERARY: in Asia (1:8)
>>Corrected Perspective on the Change of Itinerary (1:9—2:11)
>ITINERARY: Troas to Macedonia (1:12-13)
>>Corrected Perspective on Adequacy (2:14—7:4)
>ITINERARY: Macedonia and Titus's Good News (7:5-16)

Chapters 1-7 display Paul's great desire to see Titus and to
hear about the Corinthians. But Paul had more on his mind
than recounting how happy he was that they had obeyed him
in the Lord. He used his journeys, with all their hopes, fears,
and failures, to correct a lingering problem in Corinth, one
that inhibited the Corinthians from giving him the full commendation he deserved. In 6:11—7:4 he gives the reasons for
this restraint. On the basis of the good news from Titus, Paul
would proceed in chapters 8-13 to correct the remaining problems: the offering and the false apostles. Those opponents
were addressed and exposed in chapters 10-13. Chapters 12-13
also re-emphasize the itinerary—the ominous third visit.

Verses 12-13 provide a stark description of Paul's passing
up a wide-open opportunity to minister the gospel. Why did
he move on? The mystery of Titus's whereabouts caused the
apostle inner turmoil, because his concern for Titus's news
from Corinth superceded even Paul's concern for potential
converts in Troas. How could anyone claim Paul had little
concern for the Corinthians' well-being?

A first assertion of adequacy (2:14-17). Paul stressed time
and place in 2:14. He was "always" led in triumph and
transmitted the knowledge of God "in every place." That
reveals a startling contrast between Paul and the Corinthians,
who evaluated his erratic and hassled journeys as reflecting
anything but the glory of God. But this "fragrance of Christ"
(2:15) met with a divided reaction. For some, it smelled like
life; for others it was the stench of death (2:15-16).

The two groups mentioned appear in 1 Corinthians 1:18
where the perishing are used to foil the Corinthians' pride in
worldly wisdom. That life-and-death thrust also emerges in
2 Corinthians 7:10. Success in Paul's ministry was not
crowned by the numbers who were saved, or diminished by
the numbers who scoffed. The divided response may have
been used by Paul's opponents against him. But success was
being a fragrance of Christ and letting God take care of the

responses. Paul was successful before God, no matter how the Corinthians or others ultimately responded.

In 2:16 Paul asked a foundational question: "And who is adequate for these things?" The answer to that question spans the entire letter. Paul responded with two groups in view: (1) himself and his co-workers, "we"; and (2) "many" (2:17). The second group no doubt included the opponents hinted at throughout the letter. Who is adequate for this life-and-death ministry? The Corinthians were receiving two conflicting answers. Paul labored throughout to vindicate his answer; adequacy stems from pride in heart, not in appearance (5:12). He began his specific answer at this point.

Verse 17 compares and contrasts ("like" or "as" is used three times; "but" is used twice) the two groups and the problems between them. "Peddling the word of God" describes what is *not* adequate. The idea behind "peddling" is the display and promotion of a product so that it will sell. For "many" this meant slanting the gospel (4:2; 11:4) toward worldly standards of acceptability. That group is mentioned directly or indirectly in 2:17; 3:1; 4:5; 5:12; 6:14; 10:2, 7, 10; 11:12-15, 22-23; and 12:11. From this point on, the question of adequacy is resolved against the backdrop of the group that peddled the Word for profit.

Paul stressed the manner ("as," used twice in 2:17) in which he spoke rather than his content. His opponents "peddled" the Word. Paul spoke in "sincerity" (2:17); his words matched the quality of his heart. His opponents, by implication, spoke insincerely. Paul spoke "as from God," not from his own desires or schemes. He spoke "in Christ"; his words reflected only the will and character of Jesus. His critics reflected Satan (11:13-15). Finally, Paul lived in the very "sight of God." His message was always pure under God's loving and holy gaze.

The context of that speaking in Christ and the divine gaze of God stretches all the way to 12:19: "It is in the sight of God we have been speaking in Christ; and all for your upbuilding, beloved." What a wonderful description of the way to convey God's words. No wonder Paul would have to explain how he could speak of himself with such commendation and yet live such a hard life.

4

ADEQUACY IN MINISTRY COMMENDED: A SECOND DEFENSE

(3:1—5:19)

This section presents the heart of Paul's answer to the question "Who is adequate?" (2:16). Note the threefold mention of adequacy in 3:5-6. The contrasts of chapter 3 are rooted in the life-or-death reactions to his ministry (2:16). Paul used such responses to reach his goal in 5:12, to assure the Corinthians of his love and to expose true glory through the Spirit. Chapters 3-4 show the surpassing greatness of Paul's ministry, though it operated in "earthen vessels" (4:7).

NEW COVENANT ADEQUACY (3:1-11)

For Paul a cloud of personal disappointment overshadows this letter: "I have become foolish; you yourselves compelled me. Actually I should have been commended by you, for in no respect was I inferior to the most eminent apostles, even though I am a nobody" (12:11). The Corinthians should have recognized true commendation. Since they could not, Paul has to show them how.

Letters of commendation needed? (3:1-3). Some had entered Corinth with letters of commendation,[1] possibly from leaders in Jerusalem.[2] Some had also left Corinth, because

---

1. See Gerd Thiesen, *The Social Setting of Pauline Christianity* (Philadelphia: Fortress, 1982), pp. 27-67, on the social characteristics of early Christian missionaries.
2. The problem of the identity of the apostles in Jerusalem, and why they might have given their commendatory letters to these "servants of Satan" (11:14-15), is explored in R. N. Longenecker, *Paul, Apostle of Liberty* (Grand Rapids: Baker, 1976), pp. 215-16.

Paul mentioned "letters of commendation to you or from you" (3:1). Their motives were personal gain and status as they redecorated the gospel for popular consumption (2:17, "peddling"; 4:2, "adulterating the word of God"). Was Paul commending himself like the rest (3:1)?

It would appear so, but he expressly stated in 5:12 that he was not commending himself. He rejected the kind of commendation whose goal is self-exaltation and pride in externals. Nevertheless, Paul would speak quite a bit about his personal adequacy, a touchy matter that could easily be interpreted as self-serving. Perhaps for that reason, he always carefully noted that he was not qualified in and of himself, but only as a gift from God (3:5; 4:7; 10:18; 12:9; 13:7). He spoke only to glorify God and not himself (2:14; 4:5).

Paul did not deny the need to support the adequacy and excellence of his credentials. The Corinthians themselves were a letter in his heart (3:2), Paul said, which further reflected the care and comfort he felt for them. Those credentials were public (3:2), available to any who desired to check out the adequacy of his ministry. That public openness is elaborated on in 3:3; the Spirit of God wrote his letter of commendation. That exposes the basis of adequacy—credentials based on the glory of the Spirit, not on superficial glory from faint human praise. Paul was building to the great process of transformation in glory by the Spirit of God (3:18).

Any examiner would find a letter manifesting Christ, not praising Paul (3:3). Paul was a steward ("cared for") not a master, and he carried the witness of the Corinthians' spiritual growth in his heart as a letter, certifying the adequacy of his ministry. His commendation was the Spirit-caused manifestation of Christ in the lives of others. No ink and papyrus letter could match that kind of spiritual authentication. But Paul's mention of two kinds of tablets—"stone" and "heart" (3:3)—shows that he had more in mind than simple letters of reference. He was controlled by the great contrasts between the Old and New Covenants.

Covenantal contrasts (3:4-11). The first contrast in sources for adequacy is between self and God. The former is based on appearance, the latter on heart. The Corinthians had two contradictory definitions of adequacy: one from Paul and another from his opponents. Paul's confidence was based on God's work in Christ (3:4), not in himself (3:5).

The second contrast is between the Old and New Covenants (3:6). Paul describes the Old Covenant (explicitly called such in 3:14) as "stone" (3:3), "letter" (3:6), "death" (3:6-7), inferior "glory" (3:9-10), "condemnation" (3:9), and fading away (3:11). He describes the New Covenant as of "Christ" (3:3), of the "Spirit" (3:3, 6), on the "heart" (3:3), life-giving (3:6), of superior "glory" (3:8), of "righteousness" (3:9), and remaining (3:11). Here is a clear distinction between the covenants of God through Moses and Christ. The great movement from Moses to the Messiah is the heart of Paul's presentation of the gospel to the Corinthians (3:14; 4:5; see also Acts 9:22; Gal. 3:24). Three interconnected lines demonstrate the superiority of the New Covenant over the Old: (1) the superior nature of the New Covenant, (2) the resultant superior New Covenant ministry, and (3) the superior benefit for those who receive that ministry.

The superior nature of the New Covenant (3:6). Paul first takes up the issue of the nature of the covenants. The Corinthians were falling prey to an external fleshly ministry that ignored—even rejected—the glory of the inner spiritual manner of new covenant service. The letter/Spirit duality connects to the whole question of adequacy in ministry. Does adequacy come from external references or from the internal proof of the Spirit? Paul insists that his commendation came from a spiritual—and to that extent, unseen—source, unlike the showy nature of reference letters.

Here Paul is viewing the covenants from only one aspect; their modes of delivery. The Old Covenant was delivered in stone (3:7)—objective and external. The New Covenant is written on the heart—subjective and internal. Therefore, "not of the letter" (3:6) is Paul's conclusion regarding the means of delivering the New Covenant. He does not preach a covenant in words or content only. He brings a New Covenant ministry, an internal, heart-level work of the Spirit.

That new ministry of the Spirit had been predicted long ago. A careful reading of Jeremiah 31:31-34 (quoted extensively throughout Hebrews 8-10) and Ezekiel 36:22-32 shows that those Old Testament passages flooded and controlled Paul's thoughts in 2 Corinthians 3. Those passages of New Covenant glory are essential for understanding this discussion of Moses and Israel.

Paul goes on to state that "the letter kills, but the Spirit gives life" (3:6). With that, he descends from the superficial topic of references to the crucial underlying factor of any commendation: life or death results. "Letter" is any command or statement from God that a person tries to accomplish apart from the enablement of the Spirit. Content (letter alone) apart from the Spirit will only result in condemnation and death. Obviously, Paul does not assert that the Old Covenant of Moses was never coupled with the Holy Spirit. Moses (Num. 11:17) and David (Ps. 143:10)—not to mention Paul himself—speak of the Spirit in relation to the law. Paul even calls the law "spiritual" (Rom. 7:14).

But the Corinthians were falling for a ministry of externals. As a result, they were susceptible to appearance-oriented status (5:12) and were missing the perspective that viewed all things according to the new creation in Christ (5:16-17). Why Paul mentioned the two groups—those perishing and those being saved (2:15-16)—is now clarified. Rejection of Paul and his gospel came from externally forged standards.

The resultant superior New Covenant ministry (3:7-11). Paul elaborates the contrasts between the covenants to build up to his central points in 3:18 and 4:6, the two glories of ministry. The first glory is that of "the ministry of death" (3:7). Paul's descriptive phrase "in letters engraved on stones" links back to "letters of commendation" (3:1) and especially to a letter as symbolizing a mode of ministry (3:6).

The Old Testament source of Paul's discussion of Moses is Exodus 34:29-30. When Moses brought the law to Israel it came with great glory. The people had to hide their eyes from the intense reflection of God's glory on Moses' face (3:7). But Paul adds "fading as it was" to show the temporary nature of the Old Covenant as a contrast to the greater glory of "the ministry of the Spirit" (3:8). He heaps up reasons for asserting greater glory for his ministry by arguing from the lesser to the greater (3:9), by pointed overstatement (3:10), and by arguing from the lesser to the greater again (3:11). Verse 9 contrasts the result of each covenant: condemnation or righteousness. The overstatement of 3:10 is based on the glory theme, and the argument of 3:11 takes up the fading/remaining theme hinted at in 3:7.

What Paul says about the law of Moses in this section is clearly based on hindsight from the cross of Christ. The covenant at Sinai is not simply being viewed in its original setting in Moses' or David's day, but in the additional light of a New Covenant, which annulled the Old and ushered in a new age of the Spirit. The Mosaic Covenant "had glory," but in the light of the cross it "has no glory"; such is the pointed overstatement of 3:10. Paul makes extensive use of the law, basing many of his commands in this very letter on the law of Moses (3:16; 6:16; 13:1). But "ministry of death" (3:7) and "condemnation" (3:9) are strong negatives against the Mosaic Covenant, and they warrant explanation.

In view are two *ministries,* not the *contents* of the two covenants. Paul does not call the Mosaic Covenant itself condemnation and death. He keeps the content of the covenant distinct from the concept of *letter.* Here his focus is on the mode of the Word's communication: the writing of the Spirit. That mode of ministry far surpasses the great, though fading, ministry of the Old Covenant. It produces a change of heart as well as external behavior.[3]

---

3. Thomas E. Provance, " 'Who Is Sufficient for These Things?' An Exegesis of 2 Corinthians ii 15—iii 18," *Novum Testamentum* 24 (1982), pp. 62-68.

NEW COVENANT INTIMACY (3:12—4:6)

Boldness (3:12-18). Verse 12 brings Paul to a conclusion
("therefore"); verses 1-11 have been preparatory to his main
point. He spoke only from sincerity in Christ "in the sight of
God" (2:17). Such firsthand intimacy has to have its source in
the Spirit realities of the New Covenant introduced in 3:1-11.
In 3:12-18, Paul joins the "boldness" aspect of adequacy to
the theme of how the hearers respond, in this case in hardness
(3:14). That issue is based in 2:15-16 and the divided response
to the gospel.

Paul uses "great boldness" (3:12; "in our speech" is not in
the Greek). His boldness in ministry is derived from "such a
hope," as expressed in the greater glory of the New Covenant, and is the next step in teaching the Corinthians how to
recognize true adequacy (2:16). The question concerning adequacy seems to be, "Paul, if you really have an adequate and
glorious ministry from God, how can you speak so boldly
about Him and at the same time have such a lowly life-style of
rejection and weakness?" In 3:12-18, Paul replies that Spirit
realities create boldness, but that hardened rejection has
always been present in history and is a sign not of the
weakness of the speaker but of the blindness of the hearer.

That blindness is initially traced to Moses' use of a veil
(3:13). Moses put the veil on to keep the Israelites from looking "intently at the end[4] of what was fading way." He did not
want the people to stare at the final glimmers of fading glory,
but rather to realize that there was a greater nonfading glory:
the unhindered glory of God. Moses interrupted their gaze on
his own fading glory so that they could focus on the God of
unfading glory, even though they presently could not have the
direct vision that Moses alone was privileged to have. Moses
saw that direct glory when he went into the Tabernacle (Ex.

---

4. Provance, pp. 73-80. R. C. H. Lenski, *Second Epistle to the Corinthians* (Min-
    neapolis: Augsburg, 1937), p. 938, reads "end"; R. V. G. Tasker, *The Second Epistle
    of Paul to the Corinthians* (Grand Rapids: Eerdmans, 1958), p. 64, reads "goal."
    Also helpful is C. E. B. Cranfield, "St. Paul and the Law," *Scottish Journal of
    Theology* 17 (1964), pp. 57-60.

34:34), but he could only offer his people a future hope of the same vision of glory that he enjoyed firsthand. Moses' veil was a judgment on Israel's inadequate state. Their sin still blocked them from unveiled intimacy with God. The veil's periodic removal foreshadowed a future unveiled gaze on God's glory.

Paul adds an important expansion of his central point in 3:14-17. Moses interrupted the people's gaze on reflected glory. "But" (3:14) indicates that something happened by way of contrast with Moses' intentions in veiling himself. Instead of coming to understand the purpose of the veil—to refer them to the unfading glory of God Himself—"[the people's] minds were hardened." To what truth were they hardened?

First, note exactly what was fading away. In 3:7 it was the glory on Moses' face. In 3:11 it was the entire Mosaic "ministry." In 3:13 it was once again the glory on Moses' face. But in 3:14, Paul introduces "the old covenant." The covenant was read, but the hearers remained blind to the fact that its glory is finished and the New Covenant exists with greater glory. As the glory faded from the face of Moses, so it has faded from the ministry of his covenant. But a blindness has kept some from understanding that fact.

Second, notice the various positions of the veil. It was first on Moses' face (3:13), then on the hearts of the Israelites (3:14-15), and then it became synonymous with satanic blinding of the mind (4:3-4). The veil clearly becomes a broad symbol for the reason Israel (or anyone) has rejected the Messiah.

The veil symbolized blindness in two respects: (1) It hindered the beholding of glory and was thereby less than adequate as a permanent work of God, and (2) it should have prepared the mind to be alerted to the appearance of permanent, unveiled glory. The symbol involved a potential risk. The mind may have become hardened (by "the god of this world," 4:4) and blind to the permanent, being infatuated with that which is flashy but fading, a problem shared by the hearers of both Moses and Paul.

So, in Moses' day and in Paul's, a hardening force was at work, keeping some from responding to the true glory of God. Another force at work can lift the veil of blindness (3:14-15) and commence, on a personal level, the process of life "from glory to glory" (3:18). Who, indeed, is adequate for this condemning and redeeming ministry, asks Paul in 2:15-16. His first point in this section is that adequacy comes from the one who boldly speaks before God in an unveiled manner (2:17; 3:12). Only the spiritually blind will miss the manifestations of true glory. In other words, if the gospel is veiled (4:3), it is not because of inadequacy of the minister but the hardness of the hearers.

The Exodus 34:34 quotation (3:16-18). The key to Paul's point in 3:14-17 is his quotation of Exodus 34:34 (3:16). The Old Testament context concerned Moses' second appearance with the tablets of the law. His face shone in such a glorious manner that the people were afraid to come near him, no doubt because of their recent experience of God's wrath (Ex. 32). They were recalled, however, and stood before Moses while he spoke the words of the covenant. After that Moses placed the veil over his face and removed his covering only when he went before the Lord in the Tabernacle. He replaced the veil after he spoke the words of the law to the people (Ex. 34:33, 35). The crowd was dazzled (Ex. 34:35) by glory when the law was spoken, but was denied viewing the fading glory.

But Moses was able to enjoy an unhindered gaze at the Lord. When he turned to the Lord in the Tabernacle, he removed the veil. Paul sees in this removal a twofold correspondence: (1) the veil pictured the inadequate and temporary function of the Mosaic Covenant; it covered what was fading away, and (2) Moses' removal of the veil before true glory pictured what would become a privilege for all when the New Covenant was inaugurated. That truth enables Paul to broaden the subject of "turns to the Lord" (3:16) from Moses to any who would repent.

Throughout the discussion Paul stresses the mode of

ministry: letter versus Spirit (3:6). When "a man turns to the Lord" (3:16), he turns to a ministry of the Spirit. The Lord Himself became a "life-giving spirit" (1 Cor. 15:45). This Lord whom we behold is not found in a wilderness Tabernacle, but in the spiritual vision of glory in Christ. At the end of this discussion Paul labors to show that the Lord of Christian glory is the Spirit who dwells in our hearts, not in a Tabernacle.[5] The Spirit alone brings the liberty, boldness, and intimacy of divine fellowship possible in the New Covenant.

Verse 17 ends the important explanation, begun in 3:14, of how and why Israel, from Moses' time on, had missed the greater glory behind the temporal and incomplete ministry of the Old Covenant. The hardened Israelites preferred fading rather than permanent glory. Unlike Moses, who hindered the gaze of glory, Paul provides an unhindered and transforming view of the glory of God. What better commendation could the Corinthians require?

Verse 18 needs to be read directly after 3:13 to grasp the emphasis of "but we all." There is some question as to the translation of "beholding as in a mirror" (3:18). Options included "beholding" and "reflecting."[6] Given Paul's thrust of confidence (3:4), boldness (3:12), and liberty (3:17), and his focus on the glory of God reflected in the face of Moses (3:17), "reflecting"[7] is the translation that best fits the overall context (4:6 also gives the sense of light shining out from the apostle). In 3:18 Paul concludes the line of thought begun in 3:1 regarding speaking boldly (2:17; 3:12).

The entire chapter elaborates what Paul means by adequacy and sincerity in the sight of God. Although his preaching did meet with a divided response (2:15-16), and his physical state was weak and afflicted (4:1—5:10), his badge

5. F. F. Bruce, "Christ and Spirit in Paul," *Bulletin of the John Rylands University Library* 59 (1977), pp. 259-85.

6. W. F. Arndt and F. W. Gingrich, *A Greek-English Lexicon of the New Testament and Other Early Christian Literature* (Chicago: U. of Chicago, 1957), pp. 425-26.

7. Lenski, p. 948; and Alfred Plummer, *A Critical and Exegetical Commentary on the Second Epistle of St. Paul to the Corinthians* (Edinburgh: T & T Clark, 1915), p. 105.

of adequacy was the incontrovertible fact of lives trans-
formed by the hidden yet potent glory of the Spirit ("You are
our letter," 3:1).

Paul then continues to explain the hidden aspect of that
glory.

Stability in heart (4:1-15). Twice Paul says, "Therefore we
do not lose heart" (4:1, 16). Each statement is followed by a
reason they suffered no loss of heart. The first reason is
twofold: (1) God shined in their hearts (4:2-6), and (2) the
treasure of God's glory was in earthen vessels, so that the
power would be from God, not self (4:7). The second reason
extends from 4:17 through 5:10. Paul looks not at temporal
but eternal things, such as a resurrection body and the final
judgment of Christ.

A possible accusation against Paul may stand behind the
twofold mention of loss of heart. The question of his adequacy led to a criticism of his apparent weakness. Paul replies
that, in spite of much affliction on the outside, he experienced
no collapse of life or purpose where it really counts: in the
heart. That was all according to his stated purpose for this
section (5:12). This section presents a penetrating insight into
the heart of Paul and his experience of God's presence. For
Paul, loss of heart would have been like the loss of God
Himself.

Ministry and mercy are closely aligned in Paul's thought
(4:1). "This ministry" refers back to the New Covenant glory
discussed in 3:7-18. "Mercy" relates back to adequacy from
God, not self (1:3; 3:5). Paul's adequacy is based on mercy
received, not on professional expertise. For Paul, every act of
ministry is a reflection of the mercy of God's great redemption in Christ. With such potent ministry and mercy, he does
not lose heart.

Paul then gives his method of commending himself (4:2).
Negatively, he is not walking in craftiness (see 12:16), nor
adulterating (see "peddling," 2:17) the Word of God.
Positively, he manifests the truth on the level of

"conscience." All is done "in the sight of God" (see 2:17), a reference to the whole discussion of His presence and glory in chapter 3. Paul's opponents used externals to impress the flesh, not the conscience. Paul spoke to the heart, the place where one intuitively knows what is right and wrong. The mention of "adulterating the word" implies that some ("many," 2:17) were doing that. To adulterate means to water something down and therefore to present an impure product. The only apparent reason the opponents had adulterated the gospel was to gain status in Corinth and to avoid negative reactions to the gospel message, undoubtedly living well off the Corinthians all the while.

By contrast, Paul aimed his unadulterated truth at the conscience of the inner man. *Conscience* is not what other humans think about us, or how we evaluate ourselves. It is a knowledge of how God evaluates our character. Paul relied on that type of knowledge in chapters 1 and 2, where he rehearsed his known behavior and counted on the Corinthians' consciences to substantiate the truth of his claims (1:12-14; 2:4). Since the Spirit of God is resident in each believer, and since the way of the New Covenant is not in external letter but in indwelling Spirit, Paul was always careful to rely on the Spirit's convicting work to verify his commendation. One such manifestation of truth for commendation was Paul's work with the Corinthians (3:3). If they had looked at the glory of God in their lives as a result of Paul's ministry among them, their consciences would have told them that Paul was commendable.

Never lurking too far behind the scenes was the question of why Paul often met with such heavy rejection. The theme of those being saved and those perishing (2:15) arises once more (4:3-6). Why did Paul speak so often of his rejections and failures in preaching? Would that not have been grist for his opponents' mill? "And even if" (4:3) almost amounts to "So what if it is veiled?"

Verses 1-6 of chapter 4 continue the discussion of the veil begun in chapter 3. The veil on Moses' face symbolized the

Israelites' hardened blindness. Such blindness continues in Paul's day, caused by "the god of this world" (4:4). Paul answers his critics; his rejection is caused not by his strengths or weaknesses, but by Satan.

Those who reject are "perishing" (4:3). The object to which Satan blinds them is "the gospel of the glory of Christ" (4:4). There are clear connections here with Moses' ministry. Moses hindered the eyes of his people from seeing glory (3:13), but Satan hinders the mind (3:14; 4:4) from seeing the greater glory of Christ. That prepares us for the "for" of 4:5. Were the opponents claiming that Paul's quirks were hindering the gospel? Paul's explanation (4:5) makes that accusation possible. But would Satan blind minds toward a self-exalting display of Paul's abilities? No. But because Paul preached "Christ Jesus as Lord" (4:5), Satan labored to bring about rejection and hostility. The easy life of the opponents was a signal of their alignment with self-exaltation rather than Christ-exaltation (11:20, "exalts himself"). If Paul's message was rejected, it was because he preached Christ (4:5) and "the god of this world" responded in hatred (4:4).

The clear reference to Genesis 1:3 in "light shall shine out of darkness" (4:6) has several implications for Paul's argument: (1) It shows the divinely potent commission behind his preaching; (2) it shows the consistency of God, who has dispelled darkness and sin from the dawn of creation up to the present; and (3) it shows the truth of the "new creature" (5:17), which operates throughout Paul's thought—the new humanity in the glory of the new Adam (1 Cor. 15:45). But where was all this new glory? Paul appeared to be weak.

Treasure in earthen vessels (4:7-15). Paul clearly defines the difference between external weakness and internal loss of heart. "But" (4:7) introduces that crucial distinction. Paul's standards (see 3:5; 12:9) negate any claim to adequacy based on personal sufficiency. For Paul, New Covenant life moves to an entirely different plane—one that views all believers as "new creatures" in Christ (5:17). The presence of personal suffering and weakness was the very vehicle (the purpose expressed by "that," 4:7) for displaying the true power of the Spirit. If Old Covenant glory was the light on Moses' face, then New Covenant glory is the human face of Christ (4:6), seen in earthen vessels.

Note the pattern in 4:8-9: "*x,* but not *y.*" For example, "afflicted . . . but not crushed." In the light of the great New Covenant presence of the Spirit (3:18; 4:1), Paul is able to make a distinction between inner and outer depression. For most, to have problems on the outside means to have similar problems in the heart. Most who are "afflicted in every way" are "crushed" (8:8). But Paul is able to tap the power for inner strength.

Paul's claim for inward stability never ignored or underestimated the physical and psychological pain of the stresses. He was balanced; he did not downplay his pains, but neither did his external stress destroy the life of God within him. Each had a function. As he says in 4:10, "Always carrying about in the body the dying of Jesus, that the life of Jesus also may be manifested in our body." Neither death nor life should be denied or diminished.

That life and death duality reflects those perishing or being saved in 2:15 and 4:3. The weakness of the cross is ironic. To the perishing, the cross is merely a death-event to be despised and rejected. To those being saved, however, the cross is a message of life, but life that is born through atoning death. Death is always the way to life. Paul viewed his ministry as continuing the same pattern. The "dying of Jesus" (4:10) in Paul's flesh was necessary for the life to be manifested in his flesh (4:11). To reject Paul's weakness was to reject Christ's weakness, through which God redeemed the world. "So death works in us, but life in you" (4:12). Paul's close identification with Christ provided the foundation for his view of mutuality with the Corinthians. Paul was not with them as a dictator, but as a minister of the ongoing death and life of Christ, for their ultimate upbuilding.

Such an explicit ministry of weakness raises the question of potential loss of heart and faith. What kept Paul so strong of heart in a ministry that he characterized as death working within? For the answer he drew on Psalm 116:10, "I believed" (4:13). Both Paul and the psalmist had faith in God. The specific reasons for their faith differed, but the concept of trust in the middle of trial provided the link between the Old and New Testament contexts: the basis for "having the same spirit of faith" (4:13).

Paul was not discouraged, even by the workings of death. He neither ceased to proclaim the very gospel that put him in peril nor watered the message down ("adulterating," 4:2) to make it more acceptable and his life a little easier. He believed that God would raise him up, as He raised up Jesus (4:14). But all of that was not for Paul's personal piety or joy. It was a contribution to the great overarching desire of his heart: giving thanks that would abound to the glory of God (4:15; see also 1:11).

NEW COVENANT IMMORTALITY (4:16—5:10)

Why did Paul not lose heart? First, he knew the difference between the problems of an earthen vessel and the strength found in the glory within (4:1-15). Second, he looked forward to an eternal state in which a body of glory will replace the mortal body of weakness (4:16—5:10).

Strength of heart in light of eternity (4:16-18). Paul uses a strong word of conclusion when he repeats his claim that he has not lost heart (4:16). His focus then shifts to a more specific explanation of what he understands about the inner man and the just-mentioned (4:14) resurrection. He again presents the same pattern of denial accompanied by a contrasting ("but") affirmation (see 4:1-2). The contrast in 4:1-2 shows Paul's motivation for a quality ministry. Verse 16 moves to the implications of death for the inner and outer man.

His basis for coping was twofold. First, he experienced

daily renewal of his inner man, though his outer man was decaying (4:16). That amounted to a startling description of resurrection taking place within a decaying corpse. Paul's critics, and the Corinthians as a whole, shared an all-too-high regard for physical status and well-being. How could he ever have hoped to warm their hearts to viewing the outer person as quite secondary to inner renewal? Because, second, he also had a world view that linked affliction to eternal glory. According to Paul's view, the one who loses heart is the one who sees suffering as an end in itself, rather than as a means to glory. He did not look at "things which are seen, but at the things which are not seen" (4:18). That was the very perspective he labored to instill in the Corinthians throughout this section (see 5:12). The various strands of Paul's thoughts were controlled by the central concept of what is unseen and eternal: the glory of the Spirit (chap. 3), the pledge of resurrection (1:22; 5:5), and the new creation of the believer in Christ (5:17).

Physical death is no reason for losing heart (5:1-5). Paul's attitude toward the future life was fundamental to his preaching and ethical conduct on earth (see 2:16b-17; 5:9-10). "For" (5:1) links this section to the previous one, especially to the concept of "eternal" (mentioned twice in 4:17-18). What specific eternal things enabled Paul not to lose heart (4:1, 16)?

Even if his earthly tent, meaning his present mortal state, were "torn down," he had an eternal house: a glorified resurrection state. The idea of dismantling tents came from Paul's profession, which he was well-acquainted with. "Not made with hands" refers to things not of this temporal creation. There is a close word correspondence between this verse and Mark 14:58, where Jesus referred to His earthly and resurrection bodies: "I will destroy this temple made with hands, and in three days I will build another made without hands." John 2:19-21 also clarifies that.

But Paul speaks of much more than simply his own resurrection. He says that if "our [plural] house" [singular] is dismantled, "we" [plural] have a "building [singular] from God." He made a similar statement in 4:16: "our [plural] inner man" [singular]. In 5:2 he says "in this [singular] we groan [plural]," and so on throughout the section. That movement between singular and plural is not just stylistic.

In 4:7 Paul refers to individual bodies in the plural: "this treasure in earthen vessels." The use of "earthly tent," "house," and "building" in the singular refers to the corporate existence of all Christians. We all share the earthly tent of mortality. But we may also look forward to another corporate existence—the great house of heavenly immortality. This reflects Paul's consistent view of humanity collected either in Adam or in Christ.[8]

In this great—but as yet unseen—hope Paul groaned because he longed to enter his eternal home (5:2). He viewed his present state as nakedness (5:3-4). This is clear from 5:4: "We do not want to be unclothed, but to be clothed." The next phrase ("that what is mortal may be swallowed up by life") defines being clothed. Paul foresaw the great event when, either by resurrection from the dead or by living transformation, "we shall all be changed" (1 Cor. 15:51). Mortality must put on immortality, and "death will be swallowed up in victory" (1 Cor. 15:54, quoting Isa. 25:8). Paul echoed these words almost verbatim in 5:4: "in order that what is mortal may be swallowed up by life." The present state of Paul and the church was that which is mortal. To be swallowed up by life is to put on the dwelling from heaven. Paul pictured the end of the age, when God will come for His own.

But, lest any should think that Paul had only unseen hope, he stressed again the certainty that resulted from his present experience of the "Spirit as a pledge" (5:5) of coming life. This truth cuts two ways: (1) It establishes hope for those in suffering and mortality; and (2) it cautions those who assert

---

8. I am indebted on this point to E. E. Ellis, "II Corinthians V. 1-10 in Pauline Eschatology," *New Testament Studies* 6 (1959-60), pp. 211-24.

that weakness should be avoided or despised in this present life—a danger into which the Corinthians had fallen (1 Cor. 4:5, 8). Paul was totally adequate. His present weakness reflected the sufferings of Christ for redemption. His hope was based on the unseen, but certain, promise of eternal life in the new age.

Continued good courage (5:6-10). Paul's discussion of "at home" and "absent" (5:6) is defined by 5:1-5. He was "absent from the Lord" (5:6), only in the sense that his mortality had not yet been swallowed up by life (5:4). Verses 6-8 reinforce how Paul did not lose heart. He walked by faith, not by sight (5:7)—another thrust against the appearance orientation of the Corinthians. His preference was always for the fullness of immortality (4:18; 5:4); therefore, he was always of good cheer (5:8). Paul presented a fine balance. Although he certainly preferred to see the Lord, his attitude toward his present mortality was one of good courage, not loss of heart.

An overriding ambition also transcended this age and the next: pleasing the Lord (5:9-10; see also 1:12-14; 2:17; 4:1-2). Paul explained this by saying, "Whether at home or absent" (5:9). When immortality swallows up mortality—the "absent" phrase about which Paul spoke—God's pleasure will be our goal. The same is true this side of eternity. Whether in time or eternity Paul wanted to please God. The need for pleasing God is heightened this side of eternity by the expectation of standing before the judgment seat of Christ (5:10). This judgment sorts out the quality of the deeds done in the body during this mortal, unclothed state. Far from demeaning this mortality or using it for vain glory, the Corinthians were to take a lesson from the apostle and always strive to please God.

SUMMARY OF 1:3—5:10

This concludes the description of Paul's world view begun in 1:3. He had proper credentials and was worthy of the Corinthians' respect and obedience. He was not fickle in his change of itinerary; his absence reflected his hope for a re-union of joy. His adequacy rested not on external letters of commendation, but on the greater glory of the Spirit in the New Covenant ministry.

Though this glory is hidden in earthen vessels, such weakness, rather than hindering the glory of the gospel, actually confirms its Christlikeness. External suffering abounds, but with the Spirit within and immortality ahead, there is no loss of heart. Above everything stands the Judge with His appointed judgment. Until that day, all must conform to the suffering and risen Lord, not to the human dictates of status and commendation.

Paul was then ready to apply these truths directly to the Corinthians.

ADEQUACY AS AN OPPORTUNITY FOR GENUINE PRIDE (5:11-19)

Pride in appearance (5:11-15). Though the attack on Paul's ministry was external, he struggled to expose the real, internal problems. Verse 11 is central to his argument against his critics: he was always "manifest to God." Paul tried to persuade his listeners, but not for their applause. Although people were the targets of his persuasion, God alone remained the singular evaluator and gauge of his success. As Paul neared the delivery of a very cutting exhortation, he could only hope that the Corinthians' consciences would confirm his proved and loving character.

The purpose of chapters 1-7, if not of the entire letter, is revealed in 5:12. How could the Corinthians really have been "proud" of Paul in all of his "weaknesses"? He gave them such an opportunity by distinguishing between self-commendation and commendation for edification. The opponents exalted themselves (11:20). Paul spoke to give others New Covenant insight, which involves glory through weakness. This fostered appropriate pride in the apostle and rejection of the false apostles. Verse 13 elaborates ("For") and confirms this. Whether Paul was evaluated as crazy ("beside ourselves") or sane, it was all for the love of God's redeemed. Paul's life was centered on Christ, and not himself, as 5:14 explains.

What is this love of Christ (5:14) that exercised such absolute sway over the apostle? First, it is Christ's love for us. This is emphasized in the phrases "one died for all" (5:14-15) and "Him who died and rose again on their behalf" (5:15). The person who takes this love to heart responds in kind, and the love *of* Christ is met with love *for* Christ.

Second, this love controlled (5:14) and directed Paul's behavior because of its nature. Christ's death was a death "for all, therefore all died" (5:14). The reason for His death was that all should live for Him (5:15). The practical result of the Christian's corporate participation in the death of Christ is a rededication of life from self to Savior. This defines the love of Christ, upon which Paul made his rational conclusion (5:14).

In light of being loved so much, Paul could only conclude that his life had to be totally given over to the Savior and to those being saved. His whole life was controlled by this love, as he strove to help others live for Christ. His behavior was a reaction to being loved by Christ—a reaction that modeled the love of Christ.

Summary. Paul wanted the Corinthians to have a reason to be proud of the right kind of people—Paul and his associates. This pride was to be in heart, not appearance (5:12). Two explanations for the heart-level reason for pride follow (each introduced by "for," 5:13-14). Paul was only God- and other-centered (5:13). His other-centered thrust was controlled by the love of Christ, which corrects self-centered living (5:14-15).

How Paul viewed people (5:16-19). Paul then offers two conclusions ("therefore," 5:16-17). Chapter 5, verse 16, is the negative to which 5:17 is the positive. "According to the flesh" (5:16) is the same thought as "appearance" in 5:12. The perspective that limits itself to what the eyes can see and the mind can deduce is no longer part of Paul's world view.

"According to the flesh" stands opposed to being controlled by the love of Christ (5:14-15). This centers on how to evaluate and minister to people, not simply on knowing them as humans (in flesh).

The second conclusion (5:17) grows out of the first: Paul does not relate to people according to fleshly evaluations, but according to their newness as creations in Christ. This perspective has its source in the Spirit realities of the New Covenant. "In Christ" brings a total revelation, a second Genesis for human experience. The "old things" are equivalent to "according to the flesh" and "appearance." Paul does not contend that it is impossible to live according to the old things; some in Corinth were doing just that. But Paul affirms that an entirely new way of life has become open to anyone who desires to see and obey the love of Christ.

Some might say, "If all is new in my life, it certainly does not look like it!" But that itself is an evaluation according to the flesh—the very kind of appearance-oriented judgment Paul is arguing against. Yes, he still wrestled with his old body and his sinful nature. Newness in Christ does not mean freedom from external weakness or internal passions. It means having the option and power to live according to the love of Christ that reconciled the world. Just as one needs a heart-level insight to appreciate the power in the apparent weakness of the cross, so one needs the same insight to appreciate the ways of reconciling power in the weakness of ever-present human mortality.

The concept of reconciliation (5:18-19) links the conclusions issuing from a pride-in-heart appreciation of Christ to the direct plea for reconciliation in 6:1—7:3. Paul's definition of reconciliation (5:19) was expressly suited to the life setting at Corinth. "Not counting their trespasses" was exactly Paul's way with the Corinthians. Whatever would happen, there would be no split on Paul's side of the relationship.

God could have counted our sins against us. Instead, He chose to meet us in Christ. He did not sweep our wrongs under the carpet or wink at their infinite offense. Instead of giving us what we deserved, He paid infinitely for our sin in Christ, thus enabling Him to view us as forgiven and as new creations in Christ. This is a true reason to be proud of Christ.

The Lord came in all the weakness of humanity, yet only a spiritual heart-level appreciation could see the reconciling God who worked within. This ministry of reconciliation had been passed on to Paul and others (5:19). Did the Corinthians understand that the same God was then working within Paul, not counting trespasses and offering a fullness of new creation life?

5

EXHORTATIONS TO RECONCILIATION

(5:20—7:16)

GODWARD RECONCILIATION (5:20—6:10)

Reconciliation and crucifixion (5:20-21). Paul returns to the work of Christ and its influence on his life. He is not giving his own message, but God's. He makes a general statement: "We urge on behalf of Christ" (5:20; "You" is not in the Greek text). Therefore, this is Paul's general approach to all people. Verse 5:21 summarizes how the crucifixion of Christ constitutes a message of reconciliation and provides righteousness. This is the essence of grace: Christ became sin for us. The Corinthians were righteous, and they could not be urged to be reconciled. Paul's specific exhortation to the Corinthians would go in a different direction: How they would receive this infinite grace.

Specific application to the Corinthians (6:1-10). The verses in this passage should be read as one sentence. The "also" of 6:1 moves from the general ministry of reconciliation (5:20) to one specific: the reception of such grace in vain. But this long sentence describes the apostles more than the Corinthians. It may be read this way: "While we urge (6:1), we give no cause for offense (6:3), but rather commend ourselves (6:4) in endurance (6:4-10)." The major impact of 6:1-10, couched in the larger context of apostolic commendation, is to provide a single exhortation not to receive the grace of God in vain.

To receive the grace of God in vain means to deflect God's grace from its intended goals—in this case, the ongoing control of the love of Christ (5:14-15), the one who became sin for us (5:21). This concept involves much more than simple personal piety and appreciation of God's grace for internal needs. It broadens to include God's entire desire for world redemption.

This exhortation receives scriptural support from Isaiah 49:8 (6:2). Paul quotes verbatim from the mainstream of the Greek Old Testament texts. He selects a passage whose context includes Isaiah's frustration in ministering to Israel (Isa. 49:4; perhaps a hint at Paul's own frustrations with the Corinthians?). Paul interprets and applies the passage spoken so long ago by the prophet: "Behold, now is 'the acceptable time.' " The prophet promised that God would hear and help His people on a certain day.

Paul applies this passage to his own day, a time when God was offering to aid His own. If God had chosen a time to bring aid, who was man to disregard the offer or be tardy in making full use of it? Indeed, it was the thought of receiving the grace of God in vain (6:1) that prompted Paul's mention of the Old Testament passage in the first place. Therefore, he urges his readers not to turn a deaf ear to God and ignore their redemption in Christ, or receive the grace of God in vain. Having delivered this urgent plea, in the rest of this paragraph he deals with the theme of apostolic commendation.

Paul continues to reinforce his good character and credibility, but also moves to the final punch regarding the source of and reason for the Corinthians' problem. All of the descriptive verbs in 6:3-10 hinge on "we also urge" (6:1) and show the manner of the exhortation. Paul uses a variety of words to describe this manner: "in" (6:3-7a); "by," "and" (6:7b-8a); "as," "yet" (6:8b-10). These describe the servant of God (6:4) from various perspectives: external (6:4b-5), Christian graces (6:6-7), and observed and evaluated (6:8-10). The descriptions in 6:8-10 show the positive and negative responses to Paul and his associates. These show how meticulous Paul had been to receive God's grace with the greatest care in order not to discredit his ministry and to give no cause for offense (6:3).

RESTORED RELATIONSHIPS (6:11—7:16)

Perfecting holiness (6:11—7:4). Paul gave the Corinthians a foundation for pride in heart and matches this with a wide-open heart (6:11). Here, he directly identifies that their real problem lay, not with his attitudes or qualifications, but with their own inner restraint (6:12). "Affections," or inner attitudes, are equivalent to the concept of heart. The Corinthians had a heart problem, but what caused it? In 6:14—7:1 Paul gives the reason for it.

The negative prohibition of 6:14 is closely related to the plea for the readers to open up (6:13). Verse 13 and 7:2 perfectly join together in one idea: open up. From 6:14 to 7:1 a clear break is represented in Paul's thought. This interruption is not an irrelevant digression,[1] but an emphatic discussion of the heart of the Corinthians' problems: alliance with unbelievers. A look at the first and last sentences of 6:14—7:1 shows the overarching concern of this little two-part sermon: (1) Do not be bound together with unbelievers; (2) perfect holiness results from being cleansed from all defilement of flesh and spirit.

At first appearance, this prohibition seems to have almost nothing to do with the problem at hand. How did unbelievers enter the discussion? Was not Paul talking about fellowship between Christians? Yes and no. On one hand, his aim was to reestablish the wonderful fellowship between himself and the Corinthians. On the other hand, he was trying to wean them away from their very worldly attitude (also found throughout 1 Cor.). The Corinthians were full of worldly wisdom, fleshly

---

1. For a general survey of the problem see Margaret E. Thrall, "The Problem of II Corinthians VI. 14-VII. 1 in Some Recent Discussion," *New Testament Studies* 24 (1977-78), pp. 132-48.

("walking like men," 1 Cor. 3:3) frictions, and disputes over leaders, legalities, spiritual gifts, the Lord's table, and the function of women in the church. They were acting just like the unbelievers who crucified Christ (1 Cor. 2:6-8). The problems in 1 Corinthians stemmed from association with impure believers (1 Cor. 5:11) and with unbelievers (1 Cor. 6:6; 10:19-22). Paul knew that Christians must live among unbelievers. Therefore, 6:14 must mean something other than just their dwelling among unbelievers, as shown in his use of "bound together" (or, "unequally yoked," NASB margin).

To be "unequally yoked" involves believing and following a doctrine or teaching.[2] The Old Testament source for the idea of being "unequally yoked" is Deuteronomy 22:10. The adjectival form of "unequally yoked" is found in the Greek Old Testament at Leviticus 19:19. The source of such teaching is referred to many times in 2 Corinthians (2:17—3:1; 5:12; 10:2, 10, 12; 11:3-4, 12-13, 15, 18, 20, 22). False apostles had entered Corinth and begun criticizing Paul's speech (11:6), letters (10:10), personal appearance (10:10), and qualifications to be an apostle (12:11-13). Some of the Corinthians were tending to believe such lies, probably to support the continuance of the sinful ways that Paul had previously condemned (12:21). This fence-sitting attitude had to be resolved in Paul's favor, lest the Corinthians fall prey to the ministers of Satan and lose sight of true pride in the glory of the gospel.

Paul asserts, "You are not restrained by us, but you are restrained in your own affections" (6:12) and directly moves on to command, "Do not be bound together with unbelievers" (6:14). His words in 6:14—7:1 are very general, lacking the specifics for the situation at hand (see, for example, chapters 10-13). The more general nature of 6:14—7:1 may indicate that it was used for other situations as well. As a

---

2. Joseph A. Fitzmyer, "Qumran and the Interpolated Paragraph in 2 Corinthians 6, 14-7, 1," *Catholic Biblical Quarterly* 23 (1961), p. 277.

pointed exhortation to abandon the ways of unbelievers, it is appropriate for use in a variety of settings. Nowhere else did Paul call the false apostles "unbelievers," except in this passage. He gave other descriptions that were applicable to them: "lawlessness," "darkness" (6:14), "Belial" (6:15), and "idols" (6:16). "Belial" and "darkness' certainly relate to Satan and his implied darkness in 11:14.

The first quotation (6:16) closely resembles Leviticus 26:11-12 and Ezekiel 37:27. Ezekiel's context was the great process of the restoration of Israel at the end of the captivity. Ezekiel 37:15-28 speaks of the future unified and eternal restoration under David. Ezekiel 37:26 speaks of the future covenant of peace with Israel and of God's presence among the people, symbolized by His sanctuary. This divine presence became a witness to the heathen of God's sanctifying work (Ezek. 37:28). Note how closely this context aligns with Paul's statements concerning the Temple and the dwelling of God.

The broader Leviticus context contains sanctions that formally conclude the holiness code. The immediate context is the blessing of obedience (Lev. 26:3), which results in the glory of God's presence. That obedience was based in turn on redemption from Egypt and on the Sinai Covenant (Lev. 26:13). Again, the emphasis is exodus, redemption, and divine presence.

The Leviticus passage represents the best source of Paul's quotations in 6:16 for two reasons: (1) It contains "and walk among them," which is not in the Ezekiel source; (2) Leviticus 26:1 stresses the need to separate from idolatry, an association with unbelievers about which Paul protested. Also, Leviticus 26:13 says that God broke the yoke of Egypt (see "unequally yoked," 6:14) from the necks of the Israelites.

The second quotation (6:17) is Isaiah 52:11, taken from the context of the promised restoration of Israel from Babylon. Yahweh promised to provide a new Jerusalem, inhabited by people with pure hearts and hands.

The third reference (6:18) is to 2 Samuel 7:14. The Old Testament context is Nathan's oracle to David. David wished to build a house for God, but Nathan told him that God would build a house (dynasty) for David. This promise concerned Solomon and the construction of the Temple. Once again, the emphasis is on Temple and presence.

A most striking transference has taken place between Israel and the church. The Ezekiel and Leviticus passages, which promised Israel the eternal presence of God among His people, become the presence of God in His temple the church. Isaiah 52:11, which spoke of redemption from captivity and the need to leave the uncleanness of Babylon, becomes an exhortation to remain unspotted by the evils of the Corinthian culture. Solomon, the subject of 2 Samuel 7:14, becomes the elect of the church. Paul even added "and daughters" (6:18) for complete application. For Paul, the church was the new Israel; that fact enabled him to adopt these passages as promises for the church. Within this context, passages of promise for Israel are promises for the faithful of all ages, the true community of God. God's threefold promise is being fulfilled: divine presence (6:16); purity (6:17); and divine fatherhood (6:18).

These Old Testament quotations involve much more than a simple call to purity; they are structured within the framework of exodus thought. The first exodus from Egypt (Lev. 26 and context) and the second exodus from the Babylonian captivity (see Ezek. 37 and Isa. 52 contexts), both looked forward to the greatest of all releases from bondage, not from foreign political oppression, but from the mighty force of God's wrath toward human disobedience. What is more, all three quotations are called "promises" (7:1), directly relating to the Corinthians. What ought the response of the captives be upon their release into this great exodus, but a perfection of holiness?

Paul next makes a confident plea for full reconciliation

(7:2-4). He repeats his call for openness and supplies a threefold denial, addressing the opponents' charges (7:2). Paul's attitude in chapters 1-6 is illuminated in 7:3, "I do not speak to condemn you." What has he been saying that could be taken as a condemnation? Although Paul's mood was conciliatory, his subject matter dealt with ugly slurs against his character and with the Corinthians' impurity. The Corinthians could easily have missed Paul's good-will. Instead they might have heard only his serious assertions that they were open to lies (1:17), blind to true glory (chap. 3) and eternal hope (chap. 5), receiving the grace of God in vain (chap. 6), yoked to the teachings and world views of pagans (chap. 6), and not fully cleansed from the defilements of flesh and spirit (7:1). Harsh accusations!

But neither the severity of the problems nor the underlying charity of the apostle should be neglected, lest the force of either aspect be weakened. Without a severe problem in chapters 1-7, the severity of 10-13 seems highly out of place. Without a pervasive charity in chapters 1-7 the context of "the meekness and gentleness of Christ" (10:1) seems abrupt and contradictory. Seen in proper balance, chapters 1-7 emphasize Paul's charity and good-will toward the Corinthians' repentance (7:9), and chapters 10-13 emphasize the severity of the problem, though he never lost slight of ultimate edification (12:19).

The great themes of mutuality and joy (1:14, 21-22) reappear as Paul returns to the moment when he heard the good news of Corinth from Titus. He repeats his initial thrust of mutuality, "I have said before that you are in our hearts to die together and to live together" (7:3). Being in the apostle's heart was much more than a sentimental journey, however. It meant becoming a co-traveler in the great exodus from sin to eternity. The good news brought him comfort and confidence, joy in affliction (7:4). Paul has finished his lesson of pride in heart. He now turns to address the specific basis of his joy: the Corinthians' repentance from sin.

The effects of godly sorrow (7:5-16). Paul's primary focus in chapters 1-7 is the lingering need to correct the Corinthians' alignment with worldly ways. But those chapters were written with Paul's full knowledge of the readers' repentance. Next, he spoke specifically of this good news.

"For" (7:5) begins the explanation of Paul's confidence and comfort (7:3-4). We find two levels of comfort in 7:6-7: (1) Paul was comforted by the coming of his friend, Titus; (2) he was comforted "also by the comfort with which he [Titus] was comforted in you." This is a direct reflection of 1:4, "with the comfort with which we ourselves are comforted by God." The relationship Paul desired with the Corinthians had been partially realized in their longing, mourning, and zeal for the apostle (and, therefore, his true teaching, 7:7).

But Paul even couches his joy in ways defensive of his past severe exhortation. He regrets the sorrow caused by his letter (7:8). The phrase "I see that the letter caused you sorrow, though only for a while" (7:8) defines the time of and reason for Paul's regret. The time was Titus' return. The reason was the short period of sorrow. But joy replaced regret when Paul saw that the lesson was learned (7:9).

Paul speaks of suffering loss (7:9). What would be lost, and when? The same word for "suffer loss" is used by Paul in 1 Corinthians 3:15, referring to the judgment seat of Christ. The Corinthians sorrowed according to God and corrected their ways, so that they might receive reward at the judgment seat of Christ (5:10).

Paul defines two kinds of sorrow in terms of their results: (1) worldly sorrow does not produce a change of mind or heart to see things God's way, so it eventuates in death (7:10); (2) the sorrow that leads to repentance and salvation is "according to God" (emphasized three times, 7:9-11). Paul wants to communicate that what he commanded and what the Corinthians obeyed was more than a human transaction or power play. At stake was obedience to the will of God Almighty. What is more awful than one who is joyful over that which, according to God, ought to make Him sorrowful? The Corinthians had seen life God's way and sorrowed accordingly. Cleansing occurred when the Corinthians finally felt bad about the proper things. The results listed in 7:11 show the outcome of godly sorrow and underscore the severity of this particular offense.

A kind of "I knew you had it in you!" exultation is presented in 7:12-13. Like a coach who pushes his team to the limits to gain that extra inch, so Paul had inspired the Corinthians to realize what was in them: earnest desire before God. In pointed overstatement[3] Paul even says that he did not write for the offender or the offended, "but that your earnestness on our behalf might be made known to you in the sight of God" (7:12). This offense refers to the one mentioned in 2:5-11. Paul had commanded the church to discipline the offender, so in that sense he had written "for the sake of the offender." What Paul means here is that, above all, his purpose in writing transcended even the specific "matter" (7:11). His main motive was the proof of the Corinthians' commitment and zeal for God's true ministry through Paul. Would they show themselves to be innocent in the matter, or to be accomplices?

First Corinthians was written to prove their innocence, and only secondarily to deal with the offender and the offended. First Corinthians 5 shows this same community thrust, by which the offense was judged (1 Cor. 5:2, "you"; 5:6, "you"; 5:7, "you may be"). Ultimately at stake was the purity of the Body of Christ. The Corinthians responded positively to Paul, and thus he concluded, "For this reason we have been comforted" (7:13a).

The next section focuses on the joy that Titus received from the Corinthians (7:13b-16). That specific joy formed the basis for Paul's rejoicing "even much more" (7:13). For Paul,

3. Alfred Plummer, *A Critical and Exegetical Commentary on the Second Epistle of St. Paul to the Corinthians* (Edinburgh: T & T Clark, 1915), p. 224.

there was no dichotomy between reverent reception of the minister and earnest response to the message. Even at the risk of being called self-centered, Paul made such statements as 7:12. To respond to Paul was to respond to God; to respond to the critics was to respond to Satan. There was no middle ground.

Titus held a similar position (7:15). The affection of Titus abounded because of two interrelated facts: (1) the obedience of the Corinthians, and (2) how they received him with fear and trembling. Their fear was not for Titus but for the God who worked through him. That insight enabled Paul to conclude that in everything he had confidence in them (7:16). This was not overstated, or naive, confidence. It was based on past examples of proved character, but it also sought to stimulate the future continuance of good deeds.

Paul would again claim confidence in the Corinthians (9:4), at the same time he exhorted them to complete the offering. Paul's use of confidence was like that of an encouraging father. But the way in which he spoke of Titus' response showed that he was also making a transition to the issue of the Macedonians and the Jerusalem relief offering (8:1—9:15).

We find several correspondences between 7:14-17 and 8:1—9:15:

> That your earnestness on our behalf might be known to you [7:12]
> As proving through the earnestness of others the sincerity of your love also [8:8]

> Boasted to him about you [7:14]
> Our boasting about you [9:13]

> I was not put to shame [7:14]
> We [not to speak of you] should not be put to shame [9:4]

Paul's past letter was an instrument designed to prove the Corinthians' earnestness toward God and His apostle.

Similarly, Paul's use of the Macedonians would function to show the earnestness of the Corinthians' desire to help the church in Jerusalem.

6

A TEST FOR SINCERITY OF LOVE: GIVING FROM THE HEART

(8:1—9:15)

INTRODUCTION

Why did Paul wait until this point to mention the offering? He could not speak about money when he knew some of his readers, though obedient in one item, were still yoked with unbelievers in their hearts. Not only was he being condemned by the false apostles for having an erratic and uncaring ministry, he was also in the dock for being dishonest. In chapters 1-7 Paul addressed those and other issues in a caring and reconciling way. He tried to do the near impossible: to combine his personal defense and correctives for their worldliness with praise for their innocence in the matter of immorality.

STRUCTURAL OVERVIEW OF 8:1—9:15

The first exhortation is not found until 8:7: "Abound in this gracious work also." The "also" shows the nature of the exhortation: a comparison of the Corinthians with the Macedonians. A larger section (8:9—9:15) follows, laying the foundations for the proof of the Corinthians' love (8:8). Paul frames this section with the Person and work of God in Jesus Christ (8:9; 9:15). Within this framework he deals with three problems, two centering on the Corinthians and one concerning the integrity of those who would take the money to Jerusalem.

The two Corinthian problems are concerned with equality. Why should the Corinthians have to give up their money for others? What if they should need that money later on? Paul answers their questions by discussing God's long-standing emphasis on equality (8:10-15). The second problem concerns covetousness (9:6-14). Paul's readers need to learn how to give freely from the heart, trusting God to provide for their own needs. The third problem deals with the honor of the bearers of the money (8:16-24). This section represents part of the entire epistle's concern for financial matters (see 2:17; 4:2; 11:7-12; 12:13-18).

All three of those problems were related to the work begun by Titus one year past. Paul uses the Corinthians' year-old desires and the Macedonians' already proved earnestness to urge the Corinthians off the dead center of their materialism. Paul wants them to be complete in all things—from the perfection of purity and devotion (7:1; 11:3), to the specific completion of the offering (8:6), to the most general (cf. 13:9, complete in a general sense regarding Christian maturity). In chapters 1-7 Paul tests their obedience and zeal (2:9; 7:12). In chapters 10-13 he uses the same concept (10:1; 13:9, 11). Chapters 8-9 follow the same exhort-and-test pattern concerning the specifics of the offering (8:8).

THE ILLUSTRATION OF MACEDONIA (8:1-7)

Paul was full of confidence (7:16), but he was not foolish. He knew the Corinthians had several problems that still needed solutions. In one particular matter, the Corinthians had shown themselves to be Paul's supporters (7:11, 16). He saw this as a spark that could fan into a flame, bringing full reconciliation. But for the present, there was still much work to be done.

Here is a beautiful example of how one can be genuinely positive over one point, even though many other problems exist. One fault does not void all good, nor did one success blind Paul to remaining flaws. He wanted to fan the flame of success, not to douse it under a deluge of failures. This is the proper attitude of reconciliation, not of defeatism. And reconciliation ought to pervade ministry. As Paul says, "I do not speak to condemn you; for I have said before that you are in our hearts to die together and to live together" (7:3).

How did Paul motivate these people to give? His appeal in chapters 8-9, no doubt coupled with the personal work of Titus and his friends, proved successful (Rom. 15:26). What made it so? The offering was first placed in relation to God (8:1); God's gift of Himself in Christ forms the motivation and context for all Christian giving (8:9). This section begins with "the grace of God which has been given" (8:1) and ends with "thanks be to God for His indescribable gift" (9:15). "Grace" (8:1) and "thanks" (9:15) come from the same Greek word, also used in 8:4, 6-7, 9, 16, 19.

This God-oriented gift was literally identified with the Macedonians. They not only gave money, but they gave themselves (8:5). This example represents one aspect by which Paul hoped to motivate the Corinthians to give. Verse 8:2 contains two contrasts: "affliction" and "joy"; "poverty" and "wealth." The Macedonians followed Paul's own model of joy in affliction, presumably for the same reasons: the glory of the Spirit within and God's promise of immortality ahead. Their situation of deep poverty resulted "in the wealth of their liberality" (8:2).

The obvious contrast raises a question that will be answered in 8:3-5: How could the Macedonians have wealth if they lived in deep poverty? They gave from their ability (defined in 8:11-12)—that is, their giving was commensurate with their resources, small though they were. But the Macedonians also gave *beyond* their ability. They gave until it hurt. For that reason, Paul used them as a model for the Corinthians when he discussed equality and heart-level giving.

Paul next illustrated the emotional context for the Macedonians' giving: "begging us with much entreaty" (8:4). Why did they beg, and for what? They wanted to give, and Paul seemed to have allowed that. But they wanted to give more, beyond their ability or means. It is this last effort that may have caused Paul to try to put them off,[1] to which they responded by begging with much entreaty. More likely, their response simply described their "own accord" (8:3), strong to the point of begging to participate, described as the very thing that Paul had not expected (8:5). The Macedonians viewed the offering as a "favor" (the Greek word for "grace," 8:1). They did not view it as a chore, but as an act of grace; thus their high and spontaneous motivation. This explains in part how Paul could describe their offering as "the grace of God" (8:1). It also supports the idea of the gift's free nature, not resulting from Paul's dictatorial and cunning insistence, as some claimed (12:16).

The Macedonians responded to Paul's desires out of a genuine and prior commitment to God and to Paul as His apostle (8:5). "To the Lord and to us" are closely aligned in Paul's thought. He always claimed that he represented the Lord, not himself (4:5); therefore, anyone who responded to his message would be giving himself not only to the Lord, but also to the God-ordained authority vested in Paul. That is what the Macedonians had done and what Paul urged the Corinthians to do. That is why he presented that remarkable act of giving.

But if the Macedonians' giving of self should have been normal, then why did Paul say it was something for which he had not even hoped (8:5)? Evidently that was a special rededication as part of the Macedonians' process of giving. The interpretive key is "by the will of God," the same phrase with which Paul described his own apostleship (1:1). The Macedonians discerned the will of God for them in the apostle and the offering. Having given themselves to the Lord in a

---

1. Philip Edgcumbe Hughes, *Paul's Second Epistle to the Corinthians* (Grand Rapids: Eerdmans, 1962), p. 291; R. C. H. Lenski, *Second Epistle to the Corinthians* (Minneapolis: Augsburg, 1937), p. 1129; and Alfred Plummer, *A Critical and Exegetical Commentary on the Second Epistle of St. Paul to the Corinthians* (Edinburgh: T & T Clark, 1915), pp. 235-36.

special response of rededication, they were open to giving with a sacrificial zeal.

Paul made the transition and application to the Corinthians (8:6). That verse is closely connected to 8:3-5. The completion of the Macedonians' offering was beautiful. In this light, Paul urged Titus to make a similar completion with the Corinthians. His reference always traced back to the Macedonians ("also," "as well," 8:6; "also," 8:7). The ball was then in the Corinthians' court. How would they respond?

Paul began the application with a contrast ("but," 8:7). The Corinthians had not yet responded as the Macedonians had. A year-old promise lay unfulfilled. But Paul expected that they would abound in their gift because of their already present abundance in spiritual things (8:7). Paul previously praised the Corinthians' spiritual wealth in 1 Corinthians 1:5-7; those riches had not diminished. The Spirit still supplied His gifts, and He had presented Paul and his works to the Corinthians as a model for love, a fact that Paul highlighted ("in the love we inspired in you," 8:7).

Mutuality played an important role in Paul's work with people. Although his ultimate priority was his people's loving response to their Lord, Paul knew very well that loving fellowship between apostle and flock was indispensible to the ongoing work of Christ's church.

EXHORTATIONS TO SINCERE LOVE (8:8-15)

Based on divine example (8:8-11). The Corinthians might have given a knee-jerk reaction to Paul's exhortations—"Who are you to tell us we should fall in line behind you like the Macedonians?" So, Paul had to assure the Corinthians once again that he was not standing as lord and judge over them in the matter, nor was he using the Macedonians to browbeat them. "I am not speaking this as a command" (8:8)—that is, making the Macedonians' actions the divine standard of behavior. But the Corinthians themselves had made big promises to give (8:10). Paul was simply giving them the opportunity to honor their promises with action and was supplying a model to encourage their own sincerity. Paul knew that was a potentially dangerous move, since some Corinthians did not like to be submissive or to take second place. But, because they were warming to Paul once again (7:7, 12), and had been first to commence plans for this gift, Paul's wisdom dictated that his comparison would be an appropriate stimulus.

Paul was not using that example to discourage the readers, or to produce an offering as large as the Macedonians'. He wanted proof of their sincerity (8:8). The Macedonians' example should have prompted the readers to search their own hearts. Did they care about the poor? Were they earnest in their initial commitment, or did they just want to gain glory and, in the end, get by with giving as little as possible? Was anything like the Macedonians' earnestness going on in the Corinthians' hearts? But Paul's motivation transcends mere competitive impulses. He now moves to the ultimate example of sacrificial giving.

The passage from 8:9 to 9:15 begins and ends with mention of Christ as God's gift. What does the "for" (8:9) explain or illustrate? Sincerity of love is directly linked to how deeply the Corinthians appreciated what they had received in Christ. If their love was sincere it would be a response to the already received grace of Christ (see the discussion of 5:14—6:10), not just to Paul's desires or competition with the Macedonians. "The grace" links back to 8:1, 6-7. Whatever the amount of the Corinthians' gift, it must have its source and motivation in the great gift of God in Christ. The grace of the Lord is defined in 8:9 as becoming poor so that others can become rich. If the Corinthians liked Paul's compliments in 8:7, then they would also have to acknowledge the source and implications of their riches, a fact some tended to forget (1 Cor. 4:7). Would they be willing, from thankful hearts, to follow the same pattern and become a little poorer so that the Christians in Jerusalem might become a little richer? The sincerity of their love was at stake.

Chapter 8, verse 10, clearly shows the distinction Paul made between the gift and the giver. They should not only give ("do this") but should "desire to do it." He knew that they would no doubt give something. But that was not enough for the apostle of the heart; he wanted their hearts involved as well as their wallets. The two problems he deals with in this section (equality and cheerful giving) operate at the level of will and desire, not just fiscal ability. Verse 11 urges them to finish what they have begun. He only asked them to honor their promise within the limits of their ability. This leads into the discussion of equality.

Based on human equality (8:12-15). Their offering would be acceptable according to what they had, not what they did not have (8:12). Why did Paul have to say this in such a paradoxical way? Often, his statements were responses to problems raised by the Corinthians themselves. If that was the case here, Paul once more corrected a wrong conclusion about the offering. Some, instead of seeing it as an opportunity to help others, saw it as something geared to break their fiscal backs and to let the Jerusalem Christians live it up. Someone must have implied that Paul wanted them to give even what they did not have (8:12)! Paul shunned such extremes. The whole project of the offering was not designed to gouge the Corinthians so that others could live a life of ease (8:13). Paul was not out for excess; he was out for equality and followed the very pattern given by God.

Paul defined equality as the flow from ability to need (8:14). The direction of this flow is temporal. At another time, Jerusalem might have had the ability and Corinth the need. Equality is not all having the same amount. It is having basic needs met by others' ability. But how is ability defined? Paul spoke to the Corinthians of actual ability, what they could give without going into monetary ruin. Such ability is called "abundance" (twice in 8:14). In 8:14 the noun "abundance" answers to "abound" in 8:7. Abundant giving is caused by abundant spiritual presence. The Corinthians would recognize their ability to give by noting the amount they had that exceeded their basic needs. That would no doubt take them on a conscience-searching trip as each family tried to distinguish needs from wants. That was to be a weekly sojourn (1 Cor. 16:2).

But might not one who had much to give think that he needed all his goods for himself? Some apparently questioned whether such equality as Paul proposed was really God's will. But the equality Paul has in mind is based on the law of Moses (8:15), not on his own economic theories. His quotation of Exodus 16:18 mirrors a long-standing divine intention. But how is this relevant to his argument? The Old Testament context concerns the gathering of manna in the wilderness of Sinai. God had ordered that each one gather only what he and his household could eat each day. Therefore, the one who had a huge household would gather much, but not too much, or over his daily consumption. Also, the one with a small household would not gather much when compared to the large family; but he would have no lack. Both large and small families would receive their daily bread. This equality was God's plan for the needs of Israel and became a pattern for Paul's address to the church.

But we need to look more closely at what the gift of manna had to do with equality between Corinth and Jerusalem. In Exodus God did the giving; here it was to be humans. God produced equality in the wilderness; so also Christians should produce the same in the church. The example was well-chosen, because it stressed equality with regard to daily bread, the very need of the Jerusalem Christians. The question of the relative richness or poorness of an individual's private property does not enter either the Old or New Testament contexts at this point. Paul would soon raise this issue, however, by providing insight into godly giving in 9:6-15. But first he commended those who would carry the offering to Jerusalem.

COMMENDATION OF THE ADMINISTRATORS (8:16—9:5)

Motivation of Titus (8:16-17). Titus was portrayed in two

ways in chapter 8: (1) as the one who began and completed the offering (8:6), and (2) as one who took the money to Jerusalem (8:20, 23). Titus needed Paul's commendation for both duties. Paul and his team were under attack as crafty thieves (12:14-18). Paul needed to show that, when it came time to walk away from Corinth with a pouch full of money, all would be done openly and with honor.

"The same earnestness" (8:16) linked Titus's heart to Paul's. Not only did Titus share the same earnestness for the offering, but he went of his own accord (8:17). Titus was a true self-starter and was motivated first by his own desire and, second, by Paul's appeal. Paul stressed that fact to support the genuineness of Titus' ministry. They were not simply going through the motions of taking an offering. They were full of the desire to do it (8:10), the very thing Paul asked of the Corinthians (8:7). The ministers were the models.

The church appointees (8:18-24). Chapter 8, verses 18-24, outlines the qualifications and credibility of the entire group that would take the offering to Jerusalem. The first, for example, was "the brother" whose identity remains unknown to us (8:18-19).[2] He was a man of "fame" in the ministry of "the gospel," whose commendation was placed against the background of "the churches." These were not men from Paul's own circle, as the critics might have asserted, but were well-known ministers with unimpeachable public commendation. "The brother" and the rest of the group had been "appointed" for this task (8:18, 23).

"Taking precaution that no one should discredit us in our administration of this generous gift" (8:20-21) was the heart of Paul's argument for credibility in these money matters. One way Paul avoided suspicion was to have a large and well-known group from a wide geographical area (Acts 20:4).

Paul also had Scripture on his mind. There is a clear allusion to Proverbs 3:4 (from the Greek Old Testament) in 8:21.

---

2. Guesses at his identity include Luke, Barnabas, Silas, Timothy, Aristarchus, Mark, Trophimus, Titus's real brother. See Hughes, pp. 312-16 for a survey.

Paul had regard "for what is honorable not only in the sight
of the Lord, but also in the sight of men." It was not enough
for Paul to assert that he was honorable and that God knew
it; he had to present evidence for honor among people. A
look at Proverbs 3:4 may make us wonder why Paul would
have used it.

Proverbs 3:4 was used in Paul's day with reference to
priests who were in charge of deposits and withdrawals from
the Temple treasury in Jerusalem. They had an interesting
business dress: plain shirtlike robes with no cuffs. They did
not want anyone to accuse them of stuffing a few shekels into
the many folds of their garments. So they went in and out of
the money chambers barely clad. Why? Because they had
respect and honor not only before God, who would know
they were innocent no matter how elaborately they might
dress, but also before men. Paul did not use this proverb in a
far-fetched way. He used it in the way it was interpreted in his
day, with reference to money matters.[3]

Verse 22 introduces a second brother, not known to us.
Once again the emphasis is on his diversely-tested qualifications and his personal confidence in the Corinthians. The
qualifications of those Paul sent to collect the money are summarized in 8:23. Titus was on a level with Paul; the others
were *apostles* ("sent ones") "of the churches" and "a glory
to Christ." Three specifics define the glory to Christ: (1)
church-wide fame in the gospel (8:18), (2) appointment to
travel with Paul (8:19), and (3) tested diligence (8:22). All
three of these fall within the context of the offering for the
"glory of the Lord Himself" (8:19), reflecting His grace (8:1)
and gift of Christ (9:15).

This section ends on two notes: (1) Show the proof of your
love, and (2) show the reason for boasting about you. The
next passage (9:1-5) elaborates this desire of Paul. Paul said
he might come to Corinth with some Macedonians. To make

---

3. Anthony Tyrrell Hanson, *Studies in Paul's Technique and Theology*
(Grand Rapids: Eerdmans, 1974), p. 129.

sure that all would be in order, he had sent Titus and the others on ahead. Paul explained, as tactfully as possible, why he did this. The advance guard was needed because the Corinthians had dragged their feet in fiscal ministry. This would not have looked good either for Paul or for them. At the time the matter must have been kept confidential from the Macedonians and been known only to Paul's circle of ministers. When the letter became public, the Corinthians would already have proved their sincerity.

The purpose for sending the brethren (9:1-5). The sense of "it is superfluous for me to write" (9:1) is aptly caught by F. F. Bruce's paraphrase: "But there is no need for me to go on writing to you."[4] If it was unnecessary for Paul to continue, why did he? He presents a wonderful pastoral model. He assured the Corinthians that he did not need to go on, that he had no qualms about their character. But he knew that he had to remind, help, and encourage them to action. Paul knew how to encourage without assuming dictatorial command (8:8) or resorting to character insult (9:1).

He was confident that the Corinthians were ready (9:2) to give, so he did not need to go on and on encouraging them. But he did need to explain why he had sent the brethren on ahead. Corinth had been ready for one year, and its zeal had been important to stirring up the grace of God given in Macedonia (9:2).

However, Paul's boasts might not have been matched by the Corinthians' acts (9:3). The preparation of Achaia since a year ago (9:2) meant that Corinth had all but put the money in the bag. Now the moment had come when that must be done. If not, then the Corinthians would have been found unprepared. Paul very tactfully raised the fear of shame (9:4). His own shame was central (he included the Corinthians only parenthetically). This highlighted Paul's large sense of par-

---

4. F. F. Bruce, *An Expanded Paraphrase of the Epistles of Paul* (Palm Springs, Calif.: Ronald N. Haynes, 1981), p. 145.

ticipation with the Corinthians and softened the other side of the sword; the Corinthians also could be shamed.

Paul concluded ("so," 9:5) that, in light of possible shame for all concerned, he should send the brethren to arrange matters beforehand (9:5). He wanted to give them time so that their giving would not be done under pressure. He reminded them of their promise: a "bountiful gift." It was to be a "blessing" (NASB, margin), a result of free-flowing love, not something reeking of covetousness.

Paul used what might have been mistaken as an inferior scare tactic (shame) as a reason for obeying Titus. But he had made clear that reputation was vital, if the people of God were going to claim that they reflected the glory of God (see, for example, 8:21). The Corinthians had promised; Paul had not coerced. It was all in good faith that he believed their past promise, used it as a basis for boasting to the Macedonians, and then held them to their word. This was actually a compliment to the Corinthians. Paul's urging their complete follow-through was only consistent with his belief in and demand for reliability.

But Paul had yet to get to the heart of the matter. Though they needed to keep their word and maintain a good reputation, Paul knew all too well that their follow-through attempts might have been the result merely of last-minute scrambling to save face. He would have none of that, our apostle of the heart, so he provided the God-centered perspective that would avoid such phony and grudging giving. To the obligations of promise and its potential grudging response came three great principles for making giving a blessing, not a drudge.

Paul's approach in helping them complete the offering was threefold: (1) the good beginning (8:6; 9:1-2), (2) the description of the problem (8:8, 9:3-5), and (3) the solution to the problem (8:8-15). This solution is rounded out in 9:6-15.

GIVING IS SOWING (9:6)

Paul linked the concept of bountiful giving to the theme of sowing and reaping. The Greek word for "bountiful gift" (repeated in 9:5) is used twice in 9:6 for "bountifully." The word relates much more to the attitude behind the gift than to its amount. Paul also stressed how giving is to be done ("as," 9:5). The point is definitely not the more given, the more received. Paul's primary point was that giving is related to a harvest. Like any harvest, it takes time. When the farmer puts seed into the ground, he does not finish a row, look back, shrug his shoulders and say, "Well, easy come, easy go. That's the last of that seed." No. He knows that a harvest will come of the seed that is now out of sight and given away to the earth. It is not lost; it is sown.

Paul applied this truth to giving. Money given is not lost or thrown away. It is sown and will return a very special kind of harvest. The grudging Corinthians needed to realize that giving is sowing.

But 9:6 raises the question of *what* is reaped bountifully. Is it material goods, spiritual blessings, or both? Paul would answer that in 9:8-10, but first he had another principle to help the Corinthians avoid giving out of compulsion.

GIVING IS FROM THE HEART, NOT THE PURSE (9:7)

Each person should do "as he purposed in his heart" when he gave. Paul exposed the level of true giving: the heart. For Paul, the heart was closely linked to conscience. Everything he said about New Covenant ministry and interior glory of the Spirit was applied to the heart. The Corinthians' hearts one year past had warmed to the needs of the Christians in Jerusalem. But what had happened to their genuine compassion and overt promise to give? Time had a way of cooling their commitments.

"Grudgingly or under compulsion" was another way to define "affected by covetousness" (9:5). This explains why Paul wanted the Corinthians not just to do it, but to "desire" it (8:10). He wanted all giving to be an honest reflection of their true desires and feelings about the cause to which they gave. In 9:7 he quotes Proverbs 22:8 from the Greek Old Testament (Prov. 22:9 in the English and Hebrew Bibles). If God loves a cheerful giver, then the opposite must be true as well: He hates a grudging giver. God has a well-defined attitude toward the givers who feel their offering could have been better used to buy food or to have a night out on the town: displeasure. God does not desire money alone. He is after the heart (see Matt. 6:21).

GIVING ENRICHES FOR FURTHER GIVING (9:8-11)

"God is able" (9:8). He alone is the source and enabler of material blessings. But He may not always give abundance. Paul already made clear that giving is based on ability—some will have more to give, and some less. But in no way did he insinuate that being in need is a sign of unrighteousness or lack of faith. Would he have expended so much effort for the poor in Jerusalem if, at heart, they were poor simply because they were sinful and disobedient to God's claim of faith? God is able, not bound, to give material abundance. "Sufficiency in everything" (9:8) is not an end in itself. "That you may have an abundance for every good deed" (9:8) is the singular purpose for God's causing the Corinthians to prosper. Two strands of thought flow out of 9:8: abundance for every good deed and God's ability to give sufficiency in everything (9:9-11).

The quotation of Psalm 112:9 (9:9). Chapter 9, verse 9, is a quotation of Psalm 112, which speaks of the righteous man and his ability to meet others' needs. Paul's application was that when the Corinthians had abundance it was for giving to the poor. The psalm goes on to say, "His righteousness abides forever." Men might forget the deed of charity. But such a deed is righteousness before God, never to be forgotten by Him. Such deeds are produced by the one who understands the fear of the Lord (Ps. 112:1) and walks in the way of His wisdom.

Allusion to Isaiah 55:10 and Hosea 10:12 (9:10). In 9:10, Paul elaborates a second thought from 9:8: God is able to enrich. It is easy to miss the fact that Paul alludes to Isaiah

55:10 and Hosea 10:12 (from the Greek Old Testament) in this verse. Those allusions are built on Paul's use of Psalm 112:9 (9:9), with its themes of sowing, righteousness, and aiding the poor. Paul draws a parallel, comparing God's activity in agricultural and monetary matters—planting and harvesting in both.

The question of what the harvest ("reap bountifully," 9:6) is could then be answered. The harvest is righteousness, as defined by 9:9-10. Hosea used farming imagery with reference to moral living after repentance—the sowing and reaping of righteous deeds.

Isaiah used the divinely ordained processes of nature to illustrate the effectiveness of God's utterances, also within the context of repentance followed by God's promised blessing. Paul quotes the end of Isaiah 55:10. The first part of that verse concerns God as source, means, and end. The water comes down from God. The rain accomplished its purpose to make the earth bear and sprout, in order to provide food for humanity.

Paul concludes that ministering the Word of God and ministering material gifts are similar. Seed and bread are illustrations of the effectual provisions of God. The actions of God in Isaiah 55 related to the certainty of His saving work with Israel, whereas His actions in 2 Corinthians 9:10 resulted in the increase of righteous deeds done by the believers.

In summary, "God is able to make all grace abound" (9:8). This grace has two aspects: the grace of sufficiency (9:9) and the grace of abundance (9:8). The one who has sufficiency has the basic needs of his life met, but he may or may not have the ability to give (8:12). The one who has abundance is instructed regarding God's intentions in bestowing such grace. Abundance is "for every good deed" (9:8), and God will bless and multiply such community efforts of goodwill (9:10).

GIVING CAUSES THE RECIPIENTS TO GLORIFY GOD (9:11-14)

The basic promise of abundance, "enriched in everything for all liberality" is restated in 9:11, which also adds the ef-

fect on the Christian community: thanksgiving. This is explained more fully in 9:12-14, which discusses the two results
of the offering. The first is the simple meeting of "the needs
of the saints" (9:12). The second, the most fully discussed, is
the thanksgiving that comes to God (9:11, 12b-14). It is great
to be a part of something that causes someone to lift his heart
to God in thankfulness. Verse 13 tells why thanks is given as
Paul returns to the idea of "proof." In verse 8:8, he spoke of
proving the sincerity of the Corinthians' love for God and
humanity. Those who received the offering also saw this
proof and glorified God because someone had been obedient
to their "confession of the gospel of Christ" (9:13). "The
liberality of your contribution to them" is secondary. The
heart attitude of the giver is more important than what may
be given. For the receivers, the offering as a reflection of the
givers' commitment to their gospel confession is more important than what is received.

In 9:14, Paul shows another benefit from the offering. The
recipients would be full of longing and prayers for the Corinthians. This was based on the "surpassing grace of God in
you." Paul repeatedly calls the offering the "grace of God"
(8:1, 6-7, 9; 9:8). There should be no such thing as a generous
gift from a grudging giver. Paul and the recipients perceived
that the offering should reflect gracious givers, motivated by
grace in Christ.

THE HEART OF ALL GIVING: CHRIST (9:15)

Paul speaks in 9:12 of the thanks of many, which thanks
would come to God as a result of the offering. In 9:14 he
speaks of the recipients' longing prayers on behalf of the
givers. Verse 15 sums up the greater context for giving or
receiving: the great gift of God in Christ. Whether persons are
rich or poor, givers or receivers, all participate in the singular
thanksgiving to God for salvation in Christ. One may thank
God for the gift of money, but the money is just a proof of
obedience to confessing Christ. All goes back to the God who

centers His great gift in Christ—His death, resurrection, and present ministry in Spirit.

The barb for the Corinthians in all of this was not a promise that if they would give, God would give back to them a hundredfold. The text says that God was "able" (9:8), not that He *would*. The point is the responsibility that issues from financial blessing. God is able to make one abound. But such abundance is for "every good deed" (9:8), not for self-indulgent luxury. That was Paul's stark and motivating point. He spoke none of this as a command (8:8); the issue was not black and white. But he asked the Corinthians to look in their hearts and to read their feelings about giving up some of their God-given abundance. He wanted them to reconsider the genuineness of their hearts and to match honest desire with a gracious act.

7

A WARNING TO RECOGNIZE
PAUL'S AUTHORITY

(10:1-18)

INTRODUCTION

The four-chapter section 10-13 successfully holds together two seemingly contradictory attitudes: meekness and sarcasm. Paul's sarcastic attack on his opponents is clear throughout (10:1, 11:4, 8, 11, 19-21; 12:13, 16). But this strong offense is set within a context of the meekness and gentleness of Christ (10:1). The harsh and critical content must be read within the intentions of humble and temperate emotion. How can this be? Examine the goal in view. If Paul's goal had been to put down the Corinthians and justify himself, his sarcasm could not be called meek and gentle. But because his motives were for the upbuilding of the Corinthians (12:19) his words, though strong, were by way of nurture, not destruction.

Chapter 12, verse 19, must always inform the interpretation of these chapters:

> All this time you have been thinking that we are defending ourselves to you. Actually, it is in the sight of God that we have been speaking in Christ; and all for your upbuilding, beloved.

Some of Paul's words could be mistaken as defensive backlashes. The clear framework of gentleness (10:1) and upbuilding (12:19) alerts the reader to the true heart and point of this section: edification.

REQUEST FOR COMPLETE OBEDIENCE (10:1-6)

Let me avoid punishment for you (10:1-2). "Meekness of Christ" relates to our Lord's view of Himself in submission to the Father. Paul aligns himself with this attitude of the Messiah, who, though full of the Father's power, ministered to needs with meekness, in accordance with God's ordained manner of bringing salvation to earth: through weak vessels (see Matt. 5:5). In this submission to the Father's ways, the only correct ministry is through gentleness. Paul makes clear throughout the letter that his primary concern was the Corinthians' well-being, not their punishment or his personal vindication.

Paul breaks off his sentence in the last part of 10:1 to interject a description that sarcastically reflects an opponent's criticism, which had asserted a chameleon-like vacillation of Paul depending on whether he was present or absent. Some said he was meek when present, but aggressive and bold when away from the heat of the situation. This amounts to saying that Paul did not have the courage to tell people what he really thought face-to-face, but had to wait until he was out of the line of fire before he could put on his tough-guy act. That criticism may have also hinted at a dare: "Why did Paul not come to us and fight it out, instead of trying to combat his problems through letters?" But that was exactly what Paul did not want to have happen, as 10:2 and 12:20-21 clearly show. Paul reverses this criticism. He was being meek when absent and would, if necessary, be bold when present (10:1-2).

Paul resumes his request, broken off in the middle of 10:1, in 10:2. He does not want to be bold when present. Why would he want to fight with those he loved (2:3; 12:20-21)? The potential fighters are not named, but their criticism of Paul is: "some, who regard us as if we walked according to the flesh." This goes back to 1:17, which raised the issue of Paul's fleshly decisions. This was the critics' explanation of Paul's seeming inconsistencies in behavior. In order to forestall any fighting, Paul describes the nature and power of his boldness.

I can fight with divine weapons (10:3-6). Paul describes divinely powerful warfare (10:3) in three ways: (1) destroying speculations (10:5), (2) capturing thoughts (10:5), and (3) punishing disobedience (10:6). A parenthetical description of the nature of Paul's weapons is in 10:4. Verses 5-6 describe the use he made of such weapons.

Paul concedes that he walked in the flesh, but not according to the flesh (10:3). Chapters 1-5 labor this distinction. How else could Paul (or anyone) walk, except in his earthen vessel? But Paul's measure of warfare is not estimated by the abilities of the flesh (10:4). Paul's weapons are strong by God's estimate ("mighty before God," NASB, margin), not man's. Such strength is measured by ability to raze entire fortresses, not just to fight one-on-one. Therefore, Paul's war was aggressive and broke into the enemy's home base of operations (the very figure used in 11:12). But what kind of fortress could he have had in mind?

Paul explains in 10:5 that he waged war against the internal forces of the mind, the hidden yet very potent arena of spiritual battle. He specifically mentions "speculations and every lofty thing raised up against the knowledge of God." Those thoughts are producing the Corinthians' disobedience to Christ (10:6). Some believers have their thoughts taken captive by the enemy, rather than by Christ. This verse alone supplies enough reason for the inclusion and pertinence of 6:14—7:1. Also, it shows the seriousness of their worldly affections and sets the scene for Paul's words in 11:3, concerning their potential seduction away from Christ to Satan. Paul worked to wean them away from their worldliness in chapters 1-7. Here he concludes his work in the form of an eleventh-hour appeal. His mission is to raze every lofty thing raised against God. And such he will do. But he hopes that will not include members of the Corinthian church.

"Taking every thought captive to Christ" (10:5) is not a

reference to personal piety. Paul could not read minds. He referred to an aggressive community-wide ministry that listened to what was being said and waged war against ungodly thoughts. "Every thought" summarizes "speculations and every lofty thing." This is an interpersonal taking captive of doctrine. How would Paul take every thought captive to the obedience of Christ? He would simply apply the truth of the gospel to every situation in life. Paul was concerned that people thought properly about God, and he always had his antennae out for anything that smacked of another gospel. This took an immense knowledge of Scripture and sensitivity to people on Paul's part.

Verse 6 of chapter 10 may sound contradictory, unless the distinction between the Corinthians and the false apostles is kept in mind. Paul held out no hope for the opponents' change of heart; they were irrevocably ministers of Satan, and their end (that is, their eternal judgment) would match the nature and source of their actions (11:15). He expected to combat the un-Christian thoughts of the opponents, but he hoped that all the Corinthians would have separated to his side. Paul would punish all disobedience, but he hoped the Corinthians would be found obedient. The next section focuses on the specific disobedient thought that Paul attacked.

A REMINDER OF HIS SUFFICIENT AUTHORITY (10:7-11)

Verses 7-11 of chapter 10 are framed by "let him consider" (10:7) and "let such a person consider this" (10:11). Verse 7 concerns the question of Christ's relationship to Paul. That was the major long-standing problem raised by the opponents (see 13:3, 5), and it seemed to be related not to Paul's eternal destiny (whether or not he was a Christian), but rather, to his authority (10:8). The first sentence of 10:7 may be taken as a question ("Are you looking?"), as an imperative ("Look!"), or as a simple statement ("You are looking."). The imperative fits best with the exhortation at the end of the verse ("let him consider"). Paul wanted the Corinthians to look at some externals, which he would soon list, and hoped they would conclusively certify him as owned by Christ. The special sense attached to belonging to Christ relates to apostolic qualifications (see 3:1; 5:12).

"If any one" refers to any Corinthians who might have been falling for the false apostles' slander of Paul's credibility. "Just as he is Christ's, so are we" put Paul on an equal footing with them. For the sake of a starting point in the argument, Paul asserted that an observation of externals ought not to place him in an inferior position to the false claimants. But he would go on to show that he far outstripped his opponents.

Paul claimed no "shame" (10:8) in this comparison with his critics, because his authority was for upbuilding, not for creating fear (10:8; see the same idea in 13:10). He would soon list the outward things to look at for his authority, but in 10:8-11 he wanted first to reinforce the truth that his authority was for their benefit. He did not want to terrify them into obedience (10:9).

A direct quotation of the critics, differentiating between Paul's presence and his correspondence, is given in 10:10. This was an old line of argument, aimed at avoiding the truth of Paul's statements by tearing down his personal appearance and speech. This also intimated the first-hand knowledge between Paul and his critics (possible during his second visit). They had probably had one or more occasions to meet head-on. However, Paul tried to avoid face-to-face conflict, in the hope that the Corinthians would come to their senses. As a result, he came off looking weak and impotent. This may have occurred on his second visit. Paul had to depart in sorrow, leaving his critics to continue their attacks on his weakness in presence and speech.

Paul replied to this personal insult. When he arrived he would be as bold and severe as he had been in his letters (10:11). This verse must be interpreted in the light of his impending visit, not as a statement of how he had always been with the Corinthians. What letters from Paul had the false apostles seen? Possibly the lost first letter and 1 Corinthians (1 Cor. 5:9). Perhaps the opponents had arrived after Paul's second visit and were hinted at in 1 Corinthians with reference to party strife (1 Cor. 1:12), care in building upon the right foundation (1 Cor. 3:10), head coverings (1 Cor. 11:3-16), and error concerning the resurrection (1 Cor. 15:12). They also may have been responsible for the wisdom problems (1 Cor. 3:18-23).

THE PROPER SPHERE OF COMMENDATION (10:12-18)

Not according to human measure (10:12). Paul knew full well that he would have to boast foolishly (as seen in chapters 11-12), but first he stressed that he would not play the boasting game according to the ways of his critics. He would not be bold as they were (10:12). A framework of self-commendation is formed in 10:12-18. Paul would boast, but only according to the Lord's commendation (10:18). His interpretation of Jeremiah 9:24 (quoted in 10:17) pervades this section (10:12-18): "He who boasts, let him boast in the Lord."

Paul begins in verse 12 by noting the puny measures used by his critics to gauge their praise—themselves. This gives insight into the nature of their criticism. They had their own set of standards, built around their own image, not around that of the Lord. In building their praise around such limited standards, they showed themselves to be "without understanding" where true commendation lies. They passed this problem on to the Corinthians, which necessitated Paul's extensive elaborations of true commendation.

According to God's measure (10:13). The Greek word for "sphere" comes from track and field events common to the Isthmian games held only seven miles northeast of Corinth. The track had lines within which each runner had to stay during the race. Paul would not boast outside of the lines that God had drawn for his ministry, in this case, the "reaching even as far as you." Corinth was given to Paul as a field. Others could certainly minister there with his blessing, as

Apollos, Titus, and Timothy showed. But others were in view, ones who claimed an authority over Corinth that annulled Paul's original claims of authority and replaced his God-given commission for an unhindered ministry among the Corinthians (see also Acts 18:9-10).

The bounds: Not overextending (10:14). Paul was the first to come as far as Corinth. The opponents were overextending themselves, which Paul did not do. They acted like they had priority over those who had first-hand work in the evangelization of the Corinthians.

The growth: Ever extending (10:15-16). Boasting beyond measure (10:13) is made even more specific in 10:15. The opponents were boasting ''in other men's labors.'' They claimed credit for the Corinthians' spiritual abundance. Paul hoped that as the Corinthians' faith grew he would be enabled to preach the gospel to the regions beyond them (10:15) and not remain where the gospel had already been preached (10:16). But what exactly was the relationship between the growth of their faith and the enlargement of Paul's ministry?

Verse 16 clearly shows that further missionary extension into new areas was Paul's point in bringing up the distinction between himself and his critics. Even when he left Corinth, he would only go where the gospel had not been preached. His hopes for the Corinthians were that through the maturity of their faith they would help him on his way. The hopes of the false apostles could only have been to stay at Corinth as long as possible and then move on to leech off another existing Christian community, not to start a new work. Paul always operated with the hope of entering new areas, establishing solid churches, and then moving on, never going where others had labored (Rom. 15:20). He based this philosophy on Isaiah 52:15, which he quotes in Romans 15:21. The regions beyond (10:15) were Rome and Spain (Rom. 15:24).

The foundation: Boast in the Lord (10:17-18). *Commendation* is the key word for this section. It appears several times

(10:12, 18) and is nearly synonymous with *boast* (10:13, 15-17). Structurally, "commend" begins and ends the section (10:12, 18), but in the middle part "boast" replaces "commend." Although the two words are nearly synonymous, *commendation,* according to Paul, must come from outside the human realm; *boasting* is a human activity. The Lord alone must be the object of boasting and the subject of commendation. Paul boasted in the Lord and trusted in His commendation. The critics had it wrong; they both boasted in and commended themselves. This concept of boasting linked back to 1 Corinthians and the pervasive problem of boasting in human wisdom and pride. The subject of controversy and the opponents both may have changed a bit in 2 Corinthians, but the foundational problem still remained. The Corinthians were all too prone to fall for those who blew their own horns, rather than to wait for the commendation of the Lord.

Paul said in 10:8 that if he boasted he would not be put to shame. Now it is shown how Paul had nothing to be ashamed about (10:17). He boasted in the Lord, not in himself. Paul used this quotation of Jeremiah 9:24 in his last letter (1 Cor. 1:31). The same problem of self-centered boasting persisted. Paul specifically defines a solution for this in verses 10:12-16: he worked only in areas where the gospel had not been preached. Any conversions and growth would have been a direct reflection of what the Lord had done through Paul. Certainly Paul was the agent, but he recognized there was no adequacy within himself for the task (3:5). The false apostles considered themselves to be the source of blessing, in contrast to Paul, who knew where the true power and glory were.

Now, more specifically, what was the commendation of the Lord (10:18)? How did Paul or the Corinthians know he had it? Paul had already answered this in his initial discussion of commendation in chapters 2-5. The one who can claim the Lord's commendation has a ministry of life and death (2:14-17), a living letter of commendation written by the Spirit on human hearts (3:1-4), and a transparent human weakness through which the greater glory of the Spirit shines (4:1—5:10). Paul knew that he was presently commended by the Lord (his ministry showed that), but he also attempted a future thrust to commendation. Paul always had the judgment seat of Christ in mind as he thought about the Lord's commendation (5:10-12; 1 Cor. 3:12-14; "and then each man's praise will come to him from God," 1 Cor. 4:5). The judgment seat of Christ is when the Lord's commendation will be fully and publicly given to His servants. Until then, His praise is hidden and seen only indirectly in the blessings of birth and growth that He gives through the ministry of the Spirit.

8

A FOOLISH DEMONSTRATION
OF PAUL'S AUTHORITY:
EARTHLY EXAMPLES

(11:1-33)

THE PROBLEM PRECIPITATING PAUL'S FOOLISHNESS (11:1-6)

His wish and confidence (11:1). Paul wished that his
readers would "bear with" him (11:1, 4, 19-20), though he
was confident that they were doing so. The "little
foolishness" grows out of 10:12; to commend oneself is to be
without understanding, a fool. Because Paul was then going
to commend himself, he called this foolishness. When compared with 10:8 this forms a startling conclusion. Paul would
not be put to shame if he boasted because he would speak the
truth. But even though he would speak truth it would still be
foolishness. The resolution of this seeming contradiction is
found on the level of attitude. What makes something foolish
is not the truth or falsity of the boast but the self-serving attitude motivating it. Paul clarified that even his foolishness
was an act (for example, 11:16-18) and exposed the behind-
the-scenes truth (12:19). He desired edification, not self-
exaltation. But, for the present, he asked their indulgence and
was confident that he would have it.

The problem exposed and illustrated (11:2-4). The three
verses 11:2-4 provide the reason for the severe and sarcastic
nature of Paul's attack on the opponents. Paul was their
spiritual father. His godly, not self-seeking, "jealousy"
linked back to the many Old Testament references concerning

99

the jealousy of God (Ex. 20:5; Deut. 5:9; 32:16). Father and daughter formed a second image, another Old Testament theme (Deut. 32:19; 2 Kings 19:21; Isa. 62:5; Jer. 18:13; 31:4). At stake was the virginal purity of an engaged daughter—the Corinthians and Christ in an intimate relationship, awaiting the great marriage of the Lamb. These metaphors show that Paul's concerns were for his beloved family's purity, not his own prestige or self-image.

Verse 3 details the problem that caused Paul to engage in foolishness. "As the serpent deceived Eve," so other serpents had entered Corinth to deceive Paul's daughter (the Corinthian church). "Craftiness" was the means of such deception, the very accusation leveled against Paul (12:16). First Timothy 2:14 mentions a similar satanic deception. The problem centered on the "mind," whose thought formed the object of Paul's warfare (10:5). The entire letter of 2 Corinthians, and especially chapters 10-13, is full of examples of this kind of Pauline warfare. The problem was satanic influence on the Corinthians' thinking. In 2:11 Satan schemes to have them withhold love from a repentant brother. "Schemes" there is the same word for "minds" in 11:3. The Israelites' minds (also the same Greek word) were hardened (3:14). In 4:4, Paul says that "the god of this world" has blinded the minds of those perishing. In 10:5 the object of Paul's warfare is speculation and every lofty thing that blocks the knowledge of God, especially counterfeit religion.

"Simplicity" is an interesting word, translated "liberality" in 8:2; 9:11, 13. Its related word is used for purity of world view and single-mindedness of devotion (Matt. 6:22; Luke 11:34; Paul also uses it in Rom. 12:8; Eph. 6:5; and Col. 3:22.) In Corinth the thoughts raised up against the gospel were making devotion for Christ complex and impure.

The impure aspects of associating with unbelievers have been dealt with in 6:14—7:1. Satan brought things in to fuzz the issue and to make Christian devotion seem complex. Paul tried to return the Corinthians to a simplicity of devotion. The serpent promised Eve elevation to equality with God, contradicting His clear command. Likewise, the deceivers in Corinth were contradicting God's desires for "devotion to Christ" and were promising an elevated life-style, which would avoid the weakness and humility found not only in Paul, but also in Christ Himself.

Those men preached "another Jesus" and a "different gospel" than the one offered by Paul (11:4). That the Corinthians were not able to see the difference, however, formed the peril of their deception and the basis of Paul's fear (11:3). What were the other Jesus and other gospel like? They were built on "speculations" and lofty things "raised up against the knowledge of God," rather than in "obedience to Christ" (10:5). They were teachings that allowed continuance of impurity (6:14—7:1), probably under the guise of wisdom and a false view of freedom. They allowed deeds that, although done under the guise of righteousness, had the opposite end (11:15). Above all, they cut the Corinthians off from the source of true wisdom and teaching found in the apostle Paul and his associates.

The central thrust of this false teaching was clear: the opponents presented a Christianity that was devoid of the glory of the Spirit and fostered disobedience to God's ways for His children in Christ. The Corinthians' lack of discernment and ease in bearing with heresy caused Paul great anxiety. They allowed another gospel, spirit, and Jesus (11:4) and put up with the foolish and anyone who would abuse them (11:19-20).

Paul evaluates himself (11:5-6). What is most intriguing is that Paul did not raise one specific doctrinal point of contention or error against his opponents. He remained general ("another Jesus," "a different spirit," "a different gospel"), preferring to dismantle his critics' position by broad blasts at their entire project. The only specific issue that Paul addressed is introduced in 11:5: the question of why the Corinthians were reticent to accept his apostolic legitimacy, but were ready to entertain ministers of Satan. Paul explained ("for") that he was not at all inferior to the "most eminent apostles" (11:5). He solved the problem by establishing his authority, not by giving a line-by-line refutation of the false thinking fostered by his opponents. He went right to the heart of the problem; by destroying their authority he would destroy their doctrine. Context dictates that the "most eminent apostles" were the false teachers in Corinth. The "for" of 11:5 logically explains 11:4. If the most eminent apostles were the original twelve apostles, how, for example, could Paul have said that he, a trained rabbi, was unskilled in speech (11:6)? What follows is an exposition of Paul's superiority over the crafty intruders and most eminent apostles, which has a stinging and sarcastic tone.

Paul's mention of "unskilled in speech" in 11:6 shows that the criticism expressed in 10:10 ("contemptible" speech) had not been far from his mind. A preparatory digression in 10:11—11:5 has established the sphere of Paul's boasting ("in the Lord," 10:17; see 10:11-18) and pointed out the serious problem precipitating it (satanic deception, 11:1-5). Paul then returns to the issue at hand: the comparison with his opponents.

Was Paul really "unskilled[1] in speech" (11:6)? He may simply have been granting it for the sake of argument, to get on the important issue of his superiority in knowledge. Paul hit at the root of the Corinthians' gullibility: inability to see the crucial difference between medium and message, content and manner. The deceivers spoke with flair and literacy and captivated the hearers. Paul, ever the bearer of glory in an earthen vessel, reminded them that knowledge is much more important than form, content than cover. "In fact, in every way we have made this evident to you in all things" (11:6).

---

1. See William F. Arndt and F. Wilbur Gingrich, *A Greek-English Lexicon of the New Testament and Other Early Christian Literature* (Chicago: U. of Chicago, 1957), p. 371, where the layman is contrasted with a specialist; R. V. G. Tasker, *The Second Epistle of Paul to the Corinthians* (Grand Rapids: Eerdmans, 1958), p. 150, "untrained in professional rhetoric." See also Acts 4:13; 1 Cor. 14:16, 23.

The words were emphatic: "in fact," "in every way," "in all things." Did the Corinthians want rhetoric or redemptive truth? Obviously, they did not know for certain, because they were dazzled by the bravura of the false apostles. But another troublesome issue needed treatment: Why Paul did not take any money from the Corinthians for his support?

THE ISSUE OF "FREE" MINISTRY (11:7-15)

The critics exalted themselves and made slaves of the Corinthians (11:20). Paul, on the other hand, humbled himself so that the Corinthians might be exalted (11:7). This reversal on Paul's part cut across the grain of the status-seeking opponents and some of the Corinthians as well. Did not Paul's humble status impugn his legitimacy as an apostle? Would a real apostle have acted in such a lowly way? Such carping criticism ignores the incarnational truth of the Son of glory as the humble and despised Son of Man. Paul simply reflected God's pattern in Christ: power perfected in the weakness of the cross (12:9). To despise this aspect of Paul's life was to despise the ways of God in Christ (1 Cor. 1:17).

Paul preached the gospel of God to the Corinthians without charge (11:7). If they had remembered another recent letter to them, they would have understood that that was his consistent mode of operation (1 Cor. 9:12, 18, 22-23), designed to save as many people as possible. Note his use of the words "save" and "win" in 1 Corinthians 9:19-22. The Corinthians had forgotten the evangelistic reasons for Paul's freely given ministry. They viewed it as a strike against his credentials. This amounted to a you-get-what-you-pay-for accusation. Paul cost nothing, so he was worth nothing, according to that mentality. As 11:20 shows, the false apostles did not come cheaply. Paul scored a direct hit on that materialistic line of reasoning.

Paul's "free" work (11:8-11). Notice how graciously Paul took aim at such slander of the gospel. The gospel that Paul delivered may have been cost-free to the hearers, but it did cost ("robbed," 11:8) someone. It cost other churches—from Macedonia (11:9), for example—not to mention the cost of the infinite sacrifice of God's Son. Paul's burden-free ministry forms a framework for these two chapters; he begins (11:7) and ends (12:13) on the note of financial support. He stresses that he was not a burden (twice in 11:9). He concludes his argument by returning to the question of being a burden (12:13-14) and denying any change in his ways. Between the two mentions of support Paul explains his methodology (11:10-15) and boasts in his family tree and ministry experiences, both in and out of the body (11:16—12:13). The money question was not incidental. It became the framework and context for his foolish boasting to convince the Corinthians of his apostolic credentials. But close to home it was the basis of another, more damaging accusation: that Paul rejected the Corinthians' money because he did not love them (11:11; 12:15).

Somehow, the Corinthians found an insult in Paul's burden-free ministry. To be sure, Paul made his Corinthian ministry public knowledge (11:10). For Paul to have asked, "Because I do not love you?" (11:11) must have implied that some people thought he did not love them. As he ends this boasting section he asks another question concerning the same issue, "If I love you the more, am I to be loved the less?" (12:15). This was the same problem Paul addressed in chapters 1-2, where he had to convince the Corinthians that his change of itinerary reflected deep-seated care, not neglect, for them.

Why he ministered "for free" (11:12-15). Why did Paul minister for free and then boast about it? To cut off opportunity from his enemies (11:12). "Opportunity" comes from a Greek military term used both of a base of wartime operations and the "resources needed to carry through an undertaking."[2] Paul wanted to destroy the base of his critics'

---

2. Arndt and Gingrich, p. 127.

operations, their claim to being regarded just as the apostle. "The matter about which they are boasting" concerned their claim to equal authority with Paul. Paul knew that they would try to match all aspects of their lives to his own in order to undercut his unique authority. But he also knew a path they would not travel: working with their hands for their own support. And he was right. Instead of working, the critics asserted that a genuine and caring apostle would not have refused the Corinthians' gracious support. In fact, Paul and Barnabas seem to have been unique in not accepting support from their present areas of ministry (1 Cor. 9:6).

Paul had seen that the question of support was a potential sore spot early on. He implied that from his earliest work in Macedonia and Achaia he was aware of some who would try to be regarded just like him. That group, therefore, did not recently appear between the writing of 1 and 2 Corinthians.[3] It was on Paul's mind from the beginning of his ministry with the Corinthians. Paul had observed false apostles trying to make the same claims he made. Obviously he considered the implications and sought the heart of the problem with those false ministers. The problem was worldliness and material-ism, so he discerned a base of operation that they would not follow: a free ministry. Paul's ministry would undercut the opponents and prove their hearts were in the world, not in God. This tactic relates to 5:12 and Paul's efforts to give his readers a distinction between pride in appearance and that in heart.

Paul's direct, no-holds-barred exposure of his enemies is contained in 11:13-15. They were clearly boasting about being apostles of Christ. But why did Paul not come out with this

---

3. As asserted by Philip Edgcumbe Hughes, *Paul's Second Epistle to the Corinthians* (Grand Rapids: Eerdmans, 1962), pp. xvii-xviii; and Alfred Plummer, *A Critical and Exegetical Commentary on the Second Epistle of St. Paul to the Corinthians* (Edinburgh: T & T Clark, 1915), p. xviii. C. K. Barrett. *A Commentary on the Second Epistle to the Corinthians* (New York: Harper & Row), p. 6, is open to the opponents' presence in Corinth prior to 1 Corinthians.

exposure at the very beginning of the letter and say, "Corinthians, why are you troubling me and aligning yourselves with ministers of Satan?" Because Paul was always equally as interested in process as in result. He knew that to attack his opponents head-on would have been premature. The Corinthians needed some preliminary truth: how to recognize boasting in appearance versus boasting in heart (chaps. 1-5), the strong exhortation to purity of affections (chaps. 6-7), and the encouragement and confidence that pervades the whole letter. But now, with such instruction behind and his third visit ahead, Paul had to make a final attempt to capture them from Satan and for Christ.

Paul then gave a threefold description of his enemies (11:13). "False apostles" described them; they were counterfeits. "Deceitful workers" defined the nature of their work. It was motivated by and resulted in deception. They had made this same accusation against Paul (4:2; 12:16). "Disguising themselves as apostles of Christ" fully described why they were false and deceitful. Their false front of apostleship was only their means of deceiving their listeners' minds (11:3).

In 11:14-15 Paul elaborates the theme of satanic masquerade. Satan is behind the disguises of the false apostles. "An angel of light" goes back to Paul's exhortation to separation in 6:14: "What fellowship has light with darkness?" From creation to Corinth to the present, Satan has been the father of all deception and darkness. Satan appears as light, but he actually encourages fellowship with darkness. The subtleties of those false workers ought not to have been underestimated. Paul was not speaking to those who were promoting gross immorality or overtly anti-Christian teachings. They were not moving from white to black. But they were subtly involved with the grays of life. As a result, however, they were bringing the Corinthians into fellowship with darkness.

Paul concluded (11:15) that Satan's deacons followed in disguised deception, specifically, in counterfeit righteousness.

This may explain why Paul did not provide a list of specific doctrinal issues in this letter. Satan here presented no such blatant denial of the cross of Christ, such as in the debates in Galatians. Instead, he subtly insinuated his servants into positions of authority by cutting down Paul's credibility and having them boast in themselves. But Paul concluded that their end would not be according to their boasts, but according to their deeds. Paul thought of the great judgment of the God who knows the truth behind human acts. Having then identified the general problem (the preaching of "another Jesus," 11:4) and the specific problem (slanders by Satan's servants regarding Paul's free service, 11:7, 15), Paul once again took up the theme of foolishness.

FOOLISHNESS DISPLAYED (11:16-29)

Sarcastic comparison (11:16-21). In 11:16 Paul says the Corinthians should not think him foolish, but if they did they should receive him anyway. This was a different way of stating his earlier request for them to bear with him (11:1). Sarcasm reigned: "I am not a fool; but if you think I am that is OK; just keep on listening. I need your attention for a little boasting." Paul clearly disassociated himself from divine conduct (11:17). He spoke not as the Lord would. However, in attitude and intent, he worked according to the Lord (12:19). He made clear that he was acting the fool (11:16-18, 21, 23, 31; 12:1, 11, 16). By asserting that this "confidence of boasting" was foolishness and not how the Lord speaks, Paul indirectly classified his opponents' words under the same foolish category.

He associated himself with the "many" (11:18, seen earlier in 2:17) who boasted according to the flesh. Paul wanted the Corinthians to avoid the path of fleshly conduct. This concept appears many times in the letter (1:17; 5:16; 10:2-3) and gathers to it the idea of appearance versus heart (5:12). Paul turned the tables and claimed it was not he who walked and boasted according to the flesh but his critics. But Paul's goal was to convict and correct his children, not just to criticize his opponents. In this light, he turned back to how easily the Corinthians bore with insults, not only to him but even to themselves.

Boasting according to the flesh was well-received in Corinth. The Corinthians claimed great wisdom (11:19) and the discerning ability to listen to fools. Paul elaborated this more pointedly in 11:20. They allowed, apparently with approval, the intruders to enslave, to devour, to take advantage, to exalt themselves, to physically abuse. Did those things really happen, or was Paul using overstatement? If he overstated, he would have played right into the hands of his critics and would have lost the bite of his sarcasm. Therefore, each of those negative things appears to have actually happened.[4]

"Enslaves" means that the false apostles brought the Corinthians (willingly?) into bondage to their false gospel (11:4). This word is used in Galatians 2:4 for what the legalistic Christians tried to do to Paul, to bring him under the law. The word graphically describes how the Corinthians were, in fact, "bound together with unbelievers" (6:14). They should have been enslaved to Christ instead (4:5).

"Devours" relates to the Corinthians' food, drink, and hospitality being freely eaten up by the false apostles. Only true apostles had a right to eat and drink from the hospitality of others, while ministering the gospel (1 Cor. 9:4). Those false apostles were like those "who devour widows' houses" (Mark 12:40). "Takes advantage of" amounts to robbery. Paul sarcastically uses this concept in 12:16: "I took you in."

"Exalts" describes the superior place claimed by the opponents. Exalted thoughts (Paul's target in 10:5) arise from exalted men. The idea of "hits you in the face" (11:20) was common in the first century.[5] Masters and rulers often hit their inferiors, or had someone else do it for them, as in the

---

4. Barrett, p. 291.

5. N. G. L. Hammond and H. H. Scullard, eds., *The Oxford Classical Dictionary,* 2d ed. (Oxford: Oxford U., 1970), articles on "slavery," p. 995, and "torture," pp. 1081-82.

case of Paul before the high priest (Acts 23:2). Paul himself was "roughly treated" (1 Cor. 4:11) and commanded that an overseer not be one who reacts with a slap or a punch (1 Tim. 3:1).

These five descriptions were not overstatements. They were the bald actions of those whom the Corinthians were actually ready to defend and support against Paul. He deftly moved from asking the Corinthians to put up with him, foolish or not, to asserting that the fools with whom they gladly bore (11:19) were not Paul and his friends but the false apostles (11:20). Irony was in full force. The Corinthians thought that others could be fools, but certainly not those flashy and convincing visitors. The Corinthians submitted to the indignities listed by Paul, while naively believing them to come from superior Christians. How could such actions have been viewed as true apostolic wisdom and authority?

But Paul's sarcasm climaxed when he said that the shame was *his* (11:21) for being so weak by comparison! This sarcasm was designed to shake his readers out of the deceit of Satan's ministers. Could the Corinthians honestly reflect on the actions listed in 11:20 and conclude that those were the Spirit-produced actions of New Covenant glory in Christ? But Paul knew that he had to finish the full line of boasting before he could rest in the Lord and send this letter. He would be just as bold (in light of the characteristics listed in 11:20), but he had to remind them once again that he was speaking in foolishness (11:21).

Foolish boasting (11:22-29). Paul boasted in pedigree. The three questions in 11:22 show that the false teachers asserted their full Jewish heritage and questioned Paul's. Perhaps because he was born in Tarsus of Cilicia they asserted that he was part Gentile. The three classes mentioned (Hebrews, Israelites, and seed of Abraham) were nearly synonymous, covering the racial, social, and theological aspects of God's people.[6] Paul claimed that he was equal to his critics in all

---

6. Barrett, p. 293.

national, linguistic, and genealogical ways.

Paul boasted in performance. If the verse above established equality with his critics, the verses that follow far outstrip them. The intruders' claims to be "servants of Christ" (11:23) probably focused on their rough times and narrow escapes. This would explain why a long list of persecutions followed Paul's "I more so." However, since Paul clearly boasted in a different direction than his enemies (boasting in weakness, 11:30; 12:9-10), it is possible that the false apostles defined their "ministry" as servants of Christ by items with which Paul contrasted his weakness. To be sure, their claim to serve Christ, defined either by weakness or strength, implied that Paul was not similarly qualified. But Paul called them servants not of Christ but of Satan (11:15), and this must form the background for the present discussion of service to Christ.

Paul's assertion that externals showed his superior service to Christ was "insane" (11:23). This continued his clear play-acting role of sane and insane boasting in the Lord. The Corinthians had the two confused. Paul played the boasting game, not for his own status, but to show the foolishness of self-centered pride. Even so, if Paul had been forced to add up the totals of their sufferings for Christ, his sum would have far exceeded those of his competitors.

Paul loads this section with words that show abundance: "far more," "without number" (11:23); "often" (11:23, 27); "five times," "three times" (11:24-25); "frequent" (11:26); "dangers" (eight times in 11:26); "many" (11:27); "daily pressure," "all the churches" (11:28).

"Labors" (11:23) is a general word that describes the toil and effort involved, whether it be in making tents, studying, or speaking the Word. If this word focuses on self-support, it heads the list as that which showed Paul's intense commitment to Christ and the Corinthians, but which, as interpreted by his critics, also showed weakness and disqualification. Labors were one aspect of life that Paul's opponents avoided like the plague. They, by contrast, devoured and took advantage of hospitality (11:20).

Perhaps his enemies could have claimed an imprisonment or two, but Paul far exceeded even their collective jail terms (11:23). Nevertheless, how was this list building to Paul's superior qualification as a servant of Christ? Being jailed is hardly the usual foundation of character qualification. Paul had the end in mind from the beginning; he boasted in his weakness (11:30).

Paul received various kinds of physical abuse. He had innumerable general beatings, arising from rowdy crowds, disgruntled religious leaders, or criminals of the city and highway. The ever-present physical abuse made Paul all too aware of what it was like to be hit "in the face" (11:20). Such situations "often" brought him potentially to the point of death (11:23). Another kind of physical harm came from the courts of the Jewish religion (11:24). "Thirty-nine lashes" were inflicted upon someone accused of a Jewish religious offense. Paul undoubtedly was accused of heresy and blasphemy because of his preaching Jesus as the Messiah. Even more impressive is why he would have allowed himself to undergo such punishment "five times" (11:24). As an apostle of Christ he was no longer under the judgments of the Jewish courts, yet he allowed himself to be sentenced and punished five times for what was probably the same accusation. Why? What point could he have made, and how was it important to his argument at this place in the letter?

The lashings took place in the synagogue, but Paul, as a Roman citizen, could have pled his case to the civil authorities and avoided religious wrath. He did not do that. Those lashings fit under the broad heading of sufferings that showed him to be a "servant of Christ" (11:23); therefore, they served to further Christ's gospel. Paul's life was a "carrying about in the body the dying of Jesus, that the life of Jesus also may be manifested in our body" (4:10). Those five agonies of lashings were vivid representations of the "sufferings of

Christ" (1:5): an effective way to portray Christ's death and
life to the brethren whom Paul loved so dearly. Could anyone
deny that this man was a servant of Christ, or that he all but
went to the cross five times in obedience to his witness?[7]

Beatings with rods and stoning were two more kinds of
Paul's punishment (11:25). Paul was beaten with rods in
Philippi (Acts 16:22). Lashing was a Jewish punishment;
beating with rods was Roman. Once again, that punishment
would not normally have been inflicted upon a Roman
citizen. Paul did not make continual use of his Roman citizen-
ship when it came to suffering for the gospel. Jesus' death
was just as much a part of Paul's witness as was His life,
which could be seen only through the weakness of suffering
(12:9-10). "Once I was stoned" refers to another form of
Jewish punishment, this time with capital intent. This refers
to Acts 14:19. In 11:23, Paul mentions two kinds of perils:
beatings and dangers of death. His eight examples of formal
beatings, lashings, and stoning serve well enough to illustrate
the civil and religious aspects of Paul's physical suffering.
Paul now moves on to illustrate the perils of being on the
road.

Although some of these dangers clearly relate to what
makes for a true servant of Christ (preaching to his countrymen, Gentiles, and false brothers), most of these descriptions were of perils any traveler in those days might have en-
countered: robbers, city dangers, wilderness, sea, rivers
(11:26). How did these contribute to Paul's argument? They
all were part of service to Christ (11:23). Paul experienced
dangers from the city, wilderness, and sea—not as a tourist,
but as one who was on a divinely ordained mission of service.
These were not the simple misfortunes of one who took a lot
of vacations; these were sufferings accrued as ambassador-at-
large for the risen Lord.

This list presented contrasts that comprehensively covered
all other dangers: Jews and Gentiles; city, wilderness, and sea

---

7. See the excellent discussion of this in R. N. Longenecker, *Paul, Apostle
of Liberty* (Grand Rapids: Baker, 1976), pp. 247-52.

(11:26). "Dangers among false brethren" (11:26) seems to be a bit out of place. But this very disjunction reveals why it came at this point. What could have been worse than all of the dangers previously mentioned? Just one: Satan masquerading as a false brother, which had a hold on Paul's dear children in Corinth. The eight dangers all describe the perils of the apostolic commission by God to "frequent journeys" (11:26).

Paul's personal lesson from such suffering was that he should not trust in himself but in God who raises even the dead (1:9). Affliction brings the sufferer to a fork in the road: trust in self or trust in God's power. The list in 11:23-33 led the Corinthians to a similar crisis of trust. Would they follow God in His power through weakness? Paul now turns to even more personal discomforts.

Through all the above-mentioned perils Paul had to continue on with his task in labor and hardship (11:27). This meant camping where he could on his journeys, with cold, hunger, and inadequate clothing to keep him warm and dry. Paul's list of service for Christ has two sections. The part examined so far includes religious and civil persecutions (11:23-25), dangers of sea, robbers, and city (11:26), and the personal effects of such dangers (11:27). The next part of the list concerns the twenty-four-hour pressure of care for the Bride of Christ. Paul's transition between parts one and two is the "apart from" phrase (11:28).

"Apart from such external things" (11:28) has a marginal reading of apart from "the things unmentioned" (NASB). The first reading means that what Paul has just said in 11:23-27 was external and therefore secondary to the daily internal pressures of caring for the churches. Lenski concludes that the list of sufferings in 11:23-27 is to be considered not the worst part of Paul's troubles, but only "beside" the real hurts.[8] The marginal reading ("the things unmentioned") means that Paul's list of physical suffering only scratches the

8. R. C. H. Lenski, *Second Epistle to the Corinthians* (Minneapolis: Augsburg, 1937), pp. 1280-81.

surface of the quantity and detail of all that Paul had gone through. Apart from those other unmentioned items, he would go on to speak of the emotional and psychological pressures of pastoral care.

The Greek word under consideration is translated "except for" (Matt. 5:32; Acts 26:29). A literal translation of 11:28 might be "apart from the things excepted." The phrase, therefore, reveals that much existed that was not included in the list. Before moving to the most difficult part of his apostolic duties, Paul alerted the reader that his list is incomplete and will remain so. He could have gone on, but refrained. He had not only far outstripped the boastings of his opponents, but he topped it off by remarking that he had not even shared all. There is also a sense of downplaying the elements in the first two parts of the list. It is as if he says, "Apart from going on and on about these ills I want to get to the real heart of my suffering as an apostle, that which no false brother could ever claim."

What a surprise to find that this (11:28) was the heart of Paul's qualifications for being a servant of Christ. His greatest labor was the loving concern for all the churches. This pressure focused daily and directly upon him, quite unlike rivers, robbers, and dangers at sea, which only occurred sporadically. There was no let-up from this particular pressure that came from all the churches with which Paul had dealt, especially in Asia Minor, Macedonia, and Achaia. He was the center of their questions, problems, and joys, each one requiring special strategies and each one touching his heart.

"Concern" carries the idea of being divided in thought or actions, distracted in many directions. This was Martha's plight in Luke 10:41. Paul's boasting at this point carried the same intentions as those above and those to follow: to display his weakness. He did not list his dangers and concerns in order to parade his bravery or strength. That would have missed his point entirely. Rather he said, "Look at me. I am beaten, cold, hungry, soaked, jailed, and am under nonstop distraction over all the churches." In this amazing manner the thought was prepared for his next sentence.

Paul now pushed his boasting to its intended aim: boasting in weakness (11:29). Some see in this verse examples of Paul's concern.[9] He was fully empathetic with those who were "weak" or "led into sin." Another possible interpretation is that Paul did not compare himself with the weak or the trapped to identify with them but rather to excel ("far more," 11:23) above them.[10] This very thing had been his thrust throughout the section on boasting. Could a weak person be found? Paul would be equally weak! Was someone trapped? Paul said he was in a fire! This was boasting in foolishness, the very thing Paul asserted he would do (11:18, 21, 23). We must not replace the foolishness of his boasting with the introduction of pastoral empathy.

Perhaps a middle ground may be found between these two interpretive options. The close connection of 11:29 with Paul's concern for the churches favors pastoral empathy as the correct interpretation. Paul identified with the aches and pains of his flock. But the intention behind the mentions of such ecclesiastical headaches was to add support to Paul's argument of comparison and boasting. Therefore, even though compassion is part of 11:29, its function in the wider context is to assert that no false apostle could have equalled Paul in his weakness and often-tempted experiences. This interpretation conforms to the next verse, "If I have to boast, I will boast of what pertains to my weakness" (11:30). The weakness and burning that Paul felt in 11:29 must have stemmed from his own afflictions and then resulted in pastoral empathetic responses.

THE FOCUS OF BOASTING (11:30-33)

Boasting in weakness (11:30-31). Paul realized that compulsion under which the Corinthians' circumstances placed

---

9. Hughes, pp. 417-18; Plummer, p. 331.
10. Barrett, pp. 301-2; Lenski, pp. 1282-83.

him: "If I have to boast" (11:30). Though boasting was foolishness it normally centered on one's strengths and accomplishments. Paul perceived a way to boast in himself, which would ultimately be a boast in the Lord, by boasting in his weaknesses. From the world's standpoint Paul's boast list (11:22-29) had gone steadily downhill. He did not dress or travel like a V.I.P., nor did he carry out his daily administrative affairs like an executive. All he could match was one hard luck story with another.

Paul's statement "To my shame I must say that we have been weak by comparison" (11:21) was sarcastic, but true. The Corinthians did view Paul as weak. Though he went on to be bold (11:21), he was only doing it according to his weakness, which he rounded out in 11:30. All that came in between was his weakness. What, then, was his boast? "I am the weakest servant of Christ!" Such a claim sounded not only foolish, but also suspect. Could he really have been telling the truth about all those adventures? In response, Paul added a strong assertion (11:31) and one final example of persecution weakness (11:32-33).

Paul called God as his witness: in 1:23, to the reason he did not come to Corinth; in 11:11, to his love for the Corinthians; and here to his truthfulness in boasting (11:31). That clearly showed how effective his critics had been in calling Paul a liar.

An inaugural example of weakness (11:32-33). Aretas IV was king over Nabataea, whose capital was Petra, from 9 B.C. to A.D. 39/40.[11] That king was, for a short time, the father-in-law to Herod Antipas. Beginning with the reign of Caligula (A.D. 37), Aretas, because of his favor with the emperor, was given power in Damascus. During that period Aretas appointed the ethnarch of whom we read in 11:32. The date for Paul's escape may then be placed between 37-40.

This little narrative was placed between two assertions of

---

11. See Hammond & Scullard, p. 104.

the necessity of boasting (11:30; 12:1). With his statement in 11:30, Paul concludes his list of sufferings, following it with the assertion of his truthfulness. Then comes this narrative (11:32-33), which may seem to have been misplaced—stuck on as an afterthought. Looking ahead, it actually provides an excellent contrast with Paul's ascent into the third heaven (12:2),[12] but more than that, it tells of the very first persecution Paul endured for Christ. Its present location gives emphasis. It stands as the inaugural display of weakness, foreshadowing all the God-predicted (Acts 9:16) sufferings that lay ahead. Its preeminence explains its position as the capstone of Paul's trials.

An entire city was shut up, in an effort to catch one man. Luke describes how the citizens were out to kill Paul (Acts 9:24). A man who had once been in the highest circles of his nation had become a lonely figure, bobbing down a makeshift elevator (11:33), scraping against the city wall, and then fleeing into the Syrian night. What thoughts concerning the significance of this escape must have filled the mind of one who had recently returned from a three-year desert experience with the Lord? We may be sure the event remained as a prime example of the weakness of Paul, through which God manifested the aroma of Christ in every place.

12. Hughes, p. 422.

9

FURTHER "FOOLISHNESS": HEAVENLY EXAMPLES

(12:1-13)

THE NECESSITY OF BOASTING (12:1)

Paul makes a distinction between necessity and profitability. The Corinthians' desire to follow high-status leaders had caused the necessity of boasting. In 1 Corinthians they had split into leadership factions while they claimed freedom and openness. Indeed, they now were so open, so willing to be free and cosmopolitan, that they were actually being deceived by Satan (11:3). The problem was serious, beyond calm discussion. So Paul's boasting was necessary. The Corinthians would profit only by responding in obedience to the boasting's inherent sarcasm and exhortation. This distinction is very important. It will be shown that all of this was done for their profit (12:19). Their understanding of the truth of Paul's words would build them up, not the boasting itself. Paul's repeated aversion to boasting was coupled with what sounded like a grudging move onward to visions and revelations. This evidently was another area of the opponents' boasting.

THE HEAVENLY REVELATIONS (12:2-4)

Paul had a definite strategy in mentioning this particular vision. First, it was fourteen years old and would have occurred around A.D. 44, possibly when Paul was at Antioch.[1]

---

1. Philip Edgcumbe Hughes, *Paul's Second Epistle to the Corinthians* (Grand Rapids: Eerdmans, 1962), p. 430.

Why would he select such an old revelation? Had he no recent experience to relate? He did, but there was something unique and formative about this particular one, old though it was. Second, he spoke of this revelation in the third person to disassociate himself from boasting in his strength. This kind of experience would have been the dream of the false apostles. They would have milked it for all it was worth in order to increase their prestige and self-exaltation (11:20) as religious men. But this illustration formed a stark contrast with the thorn that thwarted Paul's tendency toward self-exaltation (12:7). Third, he was not permitted to tell what he heard (12:4).

Another remarkable aspect in the description of this revelation is what Paul did not know: the mode of the rapture, whether in or out of the body. This ignorance is repeated (12:2-3), as if the writer or the readers thought the fact important. Readers might wonder, at the mention of rapture (12:2, 4), if the body was actually included. Or, possibly, Paul wanted to impress his readers with his stunned awe, which blanked out any awareness of being in or out of the body.

The repetition of this concept and that of rapture ("caught up," 12:2, 4) may indicate two separate visions, one in the third heaven and the other in paradise.[2] This plurality conforms to the plurals in 12:1, 7. No article ("the") is used before "visions and revelations" in 12:1. In 12:7, having listed one or two revelations, Paul uses the article ("the" revelations) to refer back to those mentioned in 12:2-5. This favors the mention of two revelations in 12:2-5. "The revelations" of 12:7 might have included others not mentioned, but the introduction of such a conjecture tells—against the more simple conclusion—that the article refers back to the two revelations previously mentioned. The presence of two revelations also explains why Paul repeats his lack of knowledge about being in or out of the body. The question would arise for each revelation.

---

2. See Hughes, p. 435, for a survey.

The "third heaven" is the realm of God beyond the observable heavens. The Old Testament speaks of "heaven" (Deut. 10:14) and "the highest heavens" (1 Kings 8:27), clearly distinguishing two levels of heavens. Whether "the highest heavens" refers to the realm of God's abode[3] is not certain. That the highest heavens were called "from ancient times" (Ps. 68:33) may not refer to the eternal realm, but rather to their presence since creation. Psalm 68:8 indentifies the heavens as the source of rain, referring to the realm of the clouds. The "highest heavens" (Ps. 68:33), in context, are the spheres above the clouds, those of the stars. Without more examples of these terms in various contexts, a final decision is difficult. But what set this revelation off from others that Paul had received, in Corinth (Acts 18:9), Troas (Acts 16:9), or even at his conversion (Acts 9:3), was the act of being caught up (12:2, 4). This explains in part why Paul refers to fourteen-year-old revelations. We must conclude that Paul's point was not what he saw in the third heaven, but simply the momentous fact that he had been there. More information was not needed.

The second revelation was a rapture into paradise (12:3-4). Paradise is clearly the abode of God. In the New Testament the word is used in Luke 23:43, 2 Corinthians 12:4, and Revelation 2:7, all of which relate to presence with God. In the Greek Old Testament this word is primarily used of Eden (Gen. 2-3) or, secondarily, of other gardens (Isa. 1:30), but it does not appear to speak of an other-worldly abode of God. According to Revelation 2:7, the one who overcomes will eat of the tree of life in the paradise of God; thus heaven is a return to a perfected Eden.

For Paul to have been caught up to paradise implied that this garden already existed and simply awaited its establishment upon earth. In paradise Paul "heard inexpressible words," words that were not to be repeated, as the next clause shows. What he heard is not relevant. That he heard what

---

3. As Hughes, p. 433, suggests.

amounted to a secret between himself and God is directly to the point. If any false apostle claimed revelations, who among them could claim such an exceptional ("caught up") state with a message so confidential that it was hidden even from Paul's most intimate associates?

PAUL'S SPHERE OF BOASTING (12:5-10)

Paul had no problem boasting about such a privileged person (12:5), but when it came to himself he only boasted about his weaknesses. Because Paul was obviously the privileged man, what could he have meant? The key is in the phrase "on my own behalf" (12:5). He saw a sharp difference between that which made for a legitimate object of boasting in and of itself and that which edified fellow believers. The fact of his exaltation was true. It would have been foolish for Paul to have used it "on his own behalf," to cause others to stand in awe of him. Not even the angels allow themselves to be worshiped (Rev. 19:10; 22:9), a lesson sorely needed by the false opponents. Paul's aim, unlike the ministers of Satan, was to show off that which magnified the power of God and drew people closer to Him. The Corinthians were all too prone to identify themselves with impressive leaders (1 Cor. 1:12), but this had the awful effect of voiding the true power of God through the cross (1 Cor. 1:17, 25). This problem, addressed in 1 Corinthians, persisted and was fed upon by the false apostles.

Paul specifically planned that he would be credited only with what he said and did in person (12:6). He did not live on past glories or future plans. To live on past revelations would have been to inspire an admiration for himself inappropriate to God's special ministry through him. Much like our Lord who kept His glory veiled until after His resurrection (Matt. 17:9), Paul also knew God's ways were through, not around, human weakness. The Paul who received such high privilege in paradise was not the Paul to be seen and appreciated among men. Such glory was not to be grasped at. The ministerial side of Paul was all weakness. He refrained from speaking about the rest that had to remain hidden within his earthen vessel. "More than he sees in me or hears from me" would have been credit based on the telling of Paul's past revelations. Paul's reticence contrasted him with his opponents, who lived on past credentials and unprovable boastings.

The words of Paul to the Colossians apply here. There he warns them to avoid anyone who takes "his stand on visions he has seen, inflated without cause by his fleshly mind" (Col. 2:18). Paul was not above the desire to live off past credit. If any were weak, so was he (11:29). In fact he was so prone to exalt himself that God provided him with a special curb against such pride. Paul's restraint in boasting (12:6) was a direct result of this divine provision against self-exaltation.

God humbled the inherent pride in the apostle. The potential cause of Paul's pride was "the surpassing greatness of the revelations" (12:7). The implication was that Paul would have exalted himself without this "thorn in the flesh." Self-exaltation, so characteristic of the messengers of Satan (11:20), was equally potential for this messenger of God. Paul's pride problem was kept in check by a "thorn in the flesh." Conjectures abound as to the precise identity of the thorn,[4] and nearly all conclude that it was some kind of physical affliction. Hope of a conclusive identification is dim and also unnecessary. Interpretive profit is found in the purpose of the illness, not its identity. And about this purpose there is no doubt: Paul states it twice.

The thorn kept Paul from exalting himself. Not only was self-exaltation a trait of Satan's messengers (11:20), but it was also a trait of the man of lawlessness, the Antichrist (2 Thess. 2:3, the only other New Testament use of the Greek word for exaltation). The thorn was *for* the flesh, rather than *in* the flesh. If Paul's point had been to locate the thorn, he would have normally used the Greek preposition for "in." His in-

---

4. See Hughes, pp. 443-46, for conjectures that include earache, headache, pain, persecutions, impure temptations, opthalmia, epilepsy, and malaria.

tent, however, was to discuss the thorn's purpose. This supports the context of controlling Paul's fleshly tendencies to boast. In this view, "flesh" means Paul's old nature, not his physical body. There is no hint that Paul's problems with his flesh were sexual. On the contrary, he twice states (12:7) that the thorn was to keep from self-exaltation, the very malady of the Corinthians that Paul had called carnal (1 Cor. 3:3).[5]

"Buffet" is a word used in Matthew 26:67 and Mark 14:65 of soldiers beating Christ with their fists; in 1 Corinthians 4:11, of Paul's being "roughly treated"; and only again in 1 Peter 2:20, of those who sin and "are harshly treated." Satan, the one behind the messenger, tempts some to immorality (1 Cor. 7:5) and some to excessive punishment (2 Cor. 2:11), transforms himself into an angel of light (2 Cor. 11:14), hinders Paul from certain journeys (1 Thess. 2:18), leads some (1 Tim. 5:15), and receives those "delivered over" (1 Cor. 5:5; 1 Tim. 1:20). The nature of the thorn was thus given a personal (demonic) identity and evil nature. Because Paul received the highest revelations, his pride became the target of one from the lowest realms. This messenger of Satan was clearly doing God's will; Satan would not have desired Paul's pride to be quenched—quite the opposite. Satan has been given strict limits within which he works his evil and concurrently accomplishes the perfect will of God. Because Paul had just called the false apostles messengers of Satan (11:14-15), some have concluded that his thorn was the continual distress caused by his many enemies.[6]

Paul prayed three times (12:8) for the thorn's removal. This sheds great light on 1 Corinthians 10:13, where Paul asserts how God provides a "way of escape" in all temptation so "that you may be able to endure it." Endurance is the way of escape: the ability to bear up under the strain of temptation without succumbing to its power. Paul endured his great thorn for the greater endurance of his many temptations to

---

5. R. V. G. Tasker, *The Second Epistle of Paul to the Corinthians* (Grand Rapids: Eerdmans, 1958), pp. 175-77.
6. Tasker, pp. 173-74.

self-exaltation. He knew that "God is faithful, who will not allow you to be tempted beyond what you are able" (1 Cor. 10:13). This clarifies why Paul at first prayed for the thorn's removal and later ceased such prayers—he realized that such affliction was "for his flesh," a much needed corrective for his pride. This entailed a process of asking and waiting three times (12:8). Paul would not have prayed for the departure of his fleshly nature, which he knew would always plague him this side of glory (Phil. 3:21). Paul may have prayed for a lessening or cessation of the public persecution that so humiliated him, though he knew such trials were those of Christ (1:5). If the thorn was a physical illness, Paul must have asked three times for the humiliating effects to be lessened.

Exactly when God clarified the relationship of Paul's affliction to his fleshly needs is not clear (12:9). It is doubtful that the primary teaching of this passage is perseverance in prayer.[7] The focus is on Paul's weakness. He had to ask three times. Three requests and finally a direct word from God were necessary before Paul realized that he was, in reality, trying to throw away God's gift ("there was given," 12:7), a gift to keep his fleshly nature from boasting in his privileged position. Whatever the precise nature of the thorn, it met Paul's pride with a shower of humiliation. He may have been caught up to heaven twice, but at that point God kept him in the dark through three petitions. Paul, like other mortals, had to wait for God. Possibly, Paul's three requests were offered up in the pain and frustration of each of the three attacks of the satanic angel. But through two such attacks the heavens were silent. That was the atmosphere that surrounded his mention of the thrice-repeated cry for help. But no affliction of the flesh or spirit can produce spirituality on its own. Paul's thorn certainly pointed out his fleshly tendencies, but the affliction had to meet *grace* in order to have its God-intended result.

---

7. As suggested by Hughes, p. 450; and Tasker, p. 178.

The answer that finally came formed the cornerstone of Paul's view of weakness and still rang in his ears as he dictated this letter. This revelation came as a formal and impressive statement from God ("He has said," 12:9), not while Paul was in paradise, but while he was in the agony of satanic attack and the perplexity of unanswered prayer. The first part of this message, "My grace is sufficient," speaks to the issue of Paul's specific request for relief. He thought God's grace would certainly include the removal of the suffering. But God's grace is related to His sufficiency, not to the presence or absence of suffering.

Grace is all of God's saving presence in Christ through the Spirit, the comfort "in" suffering (1:5), and the fullness of promise (1:20). God's grace is present with all His gifts, even the painful ones. Paul learned that the whole of his life was the grace of God, including his weakness. His ills were not somehow outside the mainstream of God's grace, but were an integral part of it. Paul's desire to be rid of the thorn was legitimate. But in this particular instance his desire was not God's. Where God made no change, that part of Paul's life was the sufficiency of God's grace.

But Paul was not simply left with the great insight that even this thorn was part of God's sufficient grace for establishing godly living. He was given what saints through the ages long for in their prayers: the reason for the answer. "For power is perfected in weakness" (12:9). Why the mention of power, rather than—say—love, witness, the gospel, or divine will? Paul's request must have been more than simply desire to return to his physical comfort. He must have wanted the thorn removed so that he could have power to be a more effective and adequate spokesman for God. But Paul needed to have his perspective changed about what made him sufficient as an apostle.

If he had wanted divine power (12:9*b*), it would not have come through removal of his affliction. Power comes through seeing weakness as the very vehicle for manifesting the power of Christ, not through gradually eliminating mortal weaknesses. Should Paul have tried to hide his human tendency to pride? Would that have made him more adequate as an apostle? No. His sufficiency only became apparent as he plainly displayed his weaknesses and let the Spirit's glory shine through them. This is why self-exaltation is so deadly to the ministry of the gospel. It replaces God's glory with human pride. Such action is satanic masquerade. God taught Paul that divine power was not to be found by matching the heights of his visionary experience with the gradual elimination of all weakness—just the opposite. The thorn functioned as the symbol of all of Paul's weaknesses and as a floodlight on true power (Phil. 3:8-11 ought to be read in this way).

This was Paul's conclusion in 12:9: "I will rather boast about my weaknesses, that the power of Christ may dwell in me." Paul had a fleshly tendency toward self-exaltation. God supplied him with a wide variety of other weaknesses (12:10) as well as the particular thorn. Those weaknesses had a twofold effect. They showed the inadequacy of the vessel, but they also affirmed the ever-present grace and power of the Spirit within. This had been Paul's argument throughout: weaknesses show flesh to be flesh, but they also open the way to seeing true glory (1:9; 4:7, 11, 16-18). Human weaknesses force us to make a decision, either to cover them up and compensate with foolish boasting (self-exaltation), or to let the weaknesses illuminate how mortal and needy we are of the truly powerful grace of God.

"I am well content with weaknesses" (12:10) moves from the single weakness of the thorn to all of Paul's trials generally surveyed in 12:10 and more specifically mentioned in 11:23-33. This greatest of weaknesses, satanic buffeting (12:7), is symbolic of all his other trials (12:10). His thorn was not essentially different from his other problems. Daily trials, whether large or small, were not smudges on his apostolic credentials, but were the very means whereby he showed God's character and presence. Paul reminded his readers that he was speaking of the trials that arose from his travels and preaching in the gospel ministry ("for Christ's sake," 12:10). Any judgment that the gospel was a message from death to death (2:16) was due to satanic blinding (4:4) and masquerading (11:14), not to apostolic inadequacy. No wonder Paul said with such confidence of his boasting in weakness, "The God and Father of the Lord Jesus, He who is blessed forever, knows that I am not lying" (11:31). Paul simply repeated God's own revealed instruction concerning the way to true boasting and power.

THE NEEDLESSNESS OF PAUL'S "FOOLISHNESS" (12:11-13)

Paul was foolish in that he, instead of the Corinthians, was commending himself (12:11). But though he commended himself he did it according to his weaknesses, not to puff himself up. Now he returns by way of summary to his alleged inferiority that began this section; "For I consider myself not in the least inferior to the most eminent apostles" (11:5); and, "for in no respect was I inferior to the most eminent apostles" (12:11). Between 11:5 and 12:11 Paul has shown that he could only have been called inferior by someone who hid the sufficiency of God under the covering of self-exaltation. Unfortunately this was the very problem of the Corinthians; "I should have been commended by you" (12:11). Paul had all the superiority of an apostle, even though he was a nobody (12:11). He emphasizes two aspects of the apostolic ministry: signs (12:12) and general treatment (12:13). He had given the Corinthians all the valid charismatic signs of an apostle. "Signs and wonders and miracles" (12:12) is a standard way of expressing the supernatural acts bestowed by the Spirit (see John 4:48; Acts 2:22, 43). Paul does not elaborate what these signs were. His point is to note that he did them and in a certain way: "with all perseverance." He had already listed in detail the cost of such determination (11:23-33).

But, at its heart, the accusation of Paul's inadequacy was actually caused by the inferiority complex of the Corinthians themselves. Paul treated Corinth just as well as any other church (12:13), with one exception: he did not become a burden to it. The Corinthians concluded that Paul had put them in an inferior position, lacked love (11:11), or, worse, had committed a sin (11:7). Paul was full of knowledge (11:6) and power, but they interpreted his reluctance to take their money as a slam against their self-worth. To this absurd conclusion Paul had given patient exhortations throughout chapters 1-7 and, in 11:1—12:10, a most intimate look into his private reasons for boasting in weakness. But he also had reserved a few sarcastic remarks, in case some still missed the message: ''Forgive me this wrong'' (12:13)! Paul's sarcasm, however, is always set in the context of patient and careful exhortation, never as an unthinking outburst of criticism.

10

A PLEA TO AVOID
PENDING JUDGMENT

(12:14—13:14)

CONTINUED DESIRE FOR TRUE MINISTRY (12:14-18)

Two elements in 12:14 introduce the conclusion of the letter: (1) Paul was about to make his third visit, and (2) he sought the Corinthians, not their money. This second point deals with the lie that said Paul wanted their money for himself. His reason for not accepting support from the Corinthians (11:12) rested on a more intimate reason: parental relationship (12:14). Parents support their children, therefore Paul would not be a burden to the Corinthians. This relationship explained his actions and validated his love. He would spend time and money, and he himself would also be gladly spent. He allowed his personal strength and emotional resources to be drawn upon. This continued the image of a loving parent/child relationship (12:15). Only satanic influence could twist such loving actions into loveless and materialistic scheming.

But such an influence was all too prevalent in Corinth. Some said Paul's assertions of love were just a cloak to cover his schemes to bilk the Corinthians out of their money (12:16). "But be that as it may" (12:16), no matter what his critics thought, Paul would not be a burden to the people at Corinth. This resolution might have diminished his respect and love in the eyes of some, but he refused to burden them. This was an indirect slap in the faces of the false apostles—what paternal relationsip could *they* claim? Paul would continue this practice, even though some would love him less for it.

Paul next approached one of the most insidious accusations leveled in this letter: that he came with sweetness and light, but used his assistants to swindle the Corinthians out of their money. "Nevertheless, crafty fellow that I am, I took you in by deceit" (12:16). "Nevertheless," in contrast with Paul's burden-free appearance, he took them in. The Greek word for "took you in" is used in 11:20 ("takes advantage of") as a description of the false apostles. The Greek word for "crafty fellow" is not used elsewhere in the New Testament, but a related noun is found in 1 Corinthians 3:19 (a quotation from Job 5:13, with reference to people who are wise in their own eyes). The same noun is used earlier in 2 Corinthians—4:2 (where Paul denied that he walked in craftiness, doubtless an accusation of his critics, clearly seen in 12:16); and 11:3 (where the word describes Satan's craftiness in the deception of Eve). Paul sarcastically applied this satanic characteristic to himself because such was being done by his critics.

The Greek word for "to deceive" was used of "adulterating" the Word of God (4:2) and was closely linked to walking in craftiness. All the major accusations against Paul with reference to money matters are included in 12:16, which also shows the heated background behind Paul's concerns over the offering for Jerusalem in chapters 8-9.

The general mention of craftiness and deceit (12:16) is made specific in 12:17-18. The issue was Paul's "taking advantage" (12:17-18) of them "through" his assistants. The insulting image behind this accusation was that Paul was the head of a ring of itinerant hucksters moving from church to church. Paul would play the self-sacrificing servant, but his associates would follow and collect a large offering, supposedly for Jerusalem. Then they would all split up the loot and move on to the next victims.

A natural reaction to such a slander would be rage, or even physical violence, but Paul's response was spiritual—a calm but pointed reference to the facts of the case. No advantage was taken by those whom Paul sent. Specifically, Titus and the brother conducted themselves in the same way as Paul did. There was no double standard between Paul and his co-workers. This illustrated Paul's stated method of commending the truth behind his ministry: "an appeal to every man's conscience in the sight of God" (4:2).

Paul sent Titus and the brother, whose identity is not known (12:18). This verse refers to Titus's past visit (or visits) to Corinth, not his upcoming one. It probably included the visit mentioned in 8:6 when Titus began his work with the offering.[1] The questions of 12:18 relate in a general way to all of Titus's past dealings with the Corinthians.

THE PURPOSE OF THE LETTER: EDIFICATION, NOT DEFENSE (12:19-21)

The context of ministry (12:19). The first sentence of 12:19 may be read as a question (there were no punctuation marks in the Greek of Paul's day), "All this time, have you been thinking that we are defending ourselves to you?" But either by question or statement, Paul exposed the attitude with which the Corinthians had been listening to him. Because of their judgmental tendencies, they would automatically have assumed that he was appealing his case as a defendant before his judges. The noun *defense* is translated "vindication of yourselves" in 7:11 and sheds much light on Paul's use of the concept here. The Corinthians thought Paul was on the defensive, trying to vindicate himself from a wrong that he had committed. That was their mistake; he had done no wrong.

At times Paul had no hesitation about presenting a defense. He gave a defense of his apostolic rights when he appealed for material support (1 Cor. 9:3). He defended his religious conduct before his countrymen (Acts 22:1), before Felix (Acts

---

1. See the discussions in Alfred Plummer, *A Critical and Exegetical Commentary on the Second Epistle of St. Paul to the Corinthians* (Edinburgh: T & T Clark, 1915), pp. 364-65; and C. K. Barrett, *A Commentary on the Second Epistle to the Corinthians* (New York: Harper & Row, 1973), p. 325.

24:10), and even before Caesar himself (Acts 25:8, 11). But in
12:19 Paul refers to the kind of defense that would try to
cover up his mistakes and ingratiate him into the Corinthians'
favor. But there was never any of this in Paul's defenses. He
always appealed to a much higher judge than any human
court: God Himself.

Near the beginning of this letter Paul said, "But as from
sincerity, but as from God, we speak in Christ in the sight of
God" (2:17). Here he repeats this in a slightly different form:
"it is in the sight of God that we have been speaking in
Christ." Paul's continual audience and judge was God. He
always spoke in Christ, with words that reflected His
character and purpose for living and dying. This corrected a
mistaken notion on the readers' parts that they acted as
Paul's judges. The Corinthians had already acted as the final
judge. They judged "before the time" (1 Cor. 4:5) because
they wanted their praise right away, before God's time. As a
result, they gained praise only from men and not from God.

But Paul stood before no judge except God (1 Cor. 2:15-16;
4:3-4). Paul made clear that he had been speaking to this
higher court. He never spoke simply to get himself off the
hook. He spoke all for the Corinthians' "upbuilding"
(12:19). He added "beloved" to raise again the entire context
of mutuality expressed throughout chapters 1-7, especially
1:14 and 7:3. His only other mention of "beloved" in 2 Corinthians climaxed his appeal for holiness (7:1). Paul did not
stand as a defendant before judges. But, as a loving father, he
urged his children on to maturity ("completion," 13:9, 11).

The concepts of defense (12:19) and commendation (3:1;
4:2; 5:12; 6:4; 7:11; 10:11-12, 18) are closely related. Some of
the Corinthians and their false apostles defined commendation as from oneself, about oneself, and for the elevation of
personal status. In such a situation, Paul was forced to commend himself (12:11); that could easily have been understood
as just one more attempt to gain status. But throughout, Paul
labors to show that status comes from the Lord alone
(10:17-18). Both defense and commendation concern the

Lord, not oneself, and are aimed at His glory and the elevation ("upbuilding") of others.

The letter's purpose summarized (12:20-21). Paul explains ("for," 12:20) why his readers needed such remarks geared toward upbuilding. He was afraid that both he and they would experience conflict, rather than the joy hoped for in 2:2-3. Eight very unpleasant events are listed (12:20). Who would have wished for these? Each event matched with aspects of the conflict addressed throughout the letter; and they were all long-standing problems, many of which had been present when Paul wrote 1 Corinthians.[2] (They can best be arranged in four pairs.)[3] Who would not have feared to enter this situation? But Paul's fear was not the result of concern over his image of self-preservation. It arose from his intense commitment as the Corinthians' spiritual father who, like any father, desired love and joy, not rebellion and discipline, with his children.

The list is presented in a softened manner. Paul did not tell the Corinthians how bad they were; instead, he hoped that none of the problems he mentioned would be present with them.

There was another aspect to Paul's fear: his own humiliation (12:21). He may have been referring to a second humiliation ("God may humiliate me *again*"), or to his return ("When I come *again*"). Either is grammatically possible, though the nearness in the Greek of "again" with "come" issues in the simplest translation, "when I come again." God, not the Corinthians, would do the humiliating, and that in front of them all. Paul, in reference to his refusal to take support, humbled himself in order to exalt the Corinthians (11:7). His journey from Ephesus to Macedonia, with all of its physical and emotional stresses, left him humbled (7:6,

---

2. Philip Edgcumbe Hughes, *Paul's Second Epistle to the Corinthians* (Grand Rapids: Eerdmans, 1962), p. 471.

3. Plummer, p. 369.

translated "depressed"). He said he was humble ("meek," 10:1) when face to face with them.

Humiliation issues from financial needs, emotional concerns, and physical afflictions. Such humiliation may have deflated all of Paul's hopes for joy at his reunion—instead of a party, a funeral. In fact, Paul even mentions potential mourning over unrepentant Christians, the ones who—even after his corrections in 1 Corinthians—still remained hardened toward God with reference to their past sins. In view was a long-standing refusal to admit that wrong had been done.

Paul's lists of vices in 12:20-21 clearly related both to the problems addressed in 1 Corinthians and to the open-hearted pleas for holiness in 2 Corinthians 6:14—7:1. Although the three sins (impurity, immorality, and sensuality, 12:21) were closely related, they highlighted aspects of particular problems in Corinth. The three words are found together in Galatians 5:19, and the combination of two of them is found in Ephesians 4:19 and Colossians 3:5. *Impurity* is a general description (as in Rom. 6:19; see 2 Cor. 6:17 for a related word). *Immorality* is linked to sexual promiscuity in Romans 13:13. Those traits spawned an alignment with leaders who conformed to external standards and allowed one's inner evil desires to run free under the guise of Christianity. "I do not sin!" they cried, pointing to the messengers of Satan who would support their position.

Paul had warned that those who engage in immorality or idolatry "shall not inherit the kingdom of God" (1 Cor. 6:9-10). But some of the Corinthians had asserted their right to indulge in immorality (1 Cor. 5:1; 6:18) and idolatry (1 Cor. 8:10, 20:21). Such problems persisted and were supported by the false apostles. Chapter 12, verses 20-21, show the heart of the Corinthians' carnality: entrenched denials that immorality was sin. Those sins had been evident during Paul's second visit and still persisted. Some had not "repented" (12:21) at Paul's urging.

THIRD-VISIT WARNINGS (13:1-10)

Introduction. All the sarcasm and foolish boasting of

chapters 10-12 comes to an end here. Paul has wiped away, by his appeal to God's highest court, any assumption that he was defendant to their jury (12:19). One aspect of Paul's apostolic authority had always been discipline (1 Cor. 4:21; 5:3-5), but even that was for upbuilding. Even in the case of the one delivered over to Satan, the goal was "that his spirit may be saved in the day of the Lord Jesus" (1 Cor. 5:5). Paul had first urged their completion by gentle instruction, then by more pointed exhortations. His third visit would bring talking to an end. In chapters 1-12 Paul hoped that he would be able to come and find obedience. In 13:1-10 he vows he will come and punish disobedience.

Warning (13:1-3). Paul again mentions his third visit and then quotes from Deuteronomy 19:15: "Every fact is to be confirmed by the testimony of two or three witnesses" (13:1). This quotation had become idiomatic and therefore is found including more (Matt. 18:16) or fewer (1 Tim. 5:19) words from the Old Testament original. But the primary question concerns why Paul used the Old Testament reference. Did he equate his three visits with the three witnesses mentioned in the quotation? But one person could represent only one witness no matter how many times he visited. However, there is support for a single witness's viewing an act on three separate occasions. Each time would be noted and on the third occurrence a conviction could then be brought.[4] But the evidence from mainline rabbinic sources supports the traditional necessity of three individuals who witness an act.[5]

The link between "third time" (see also 12:14) and "three witnesses" cannot be denied. But the link is not interpretive. The three witnesses do not equal the three visits. The question of *who* the witnesses were and *what* was witnessed must arise.

---

4. Lawrence H. Schiffman, "The Qumran Law of Testimony, " *Revue de Qumran* 8 (1975), pp. 604-5.
5. Herbert Danby, *The Mishnah* (Oxford: Oxford U. 1972), p. 299 (Sotah 6:3); Jacob Z. Lauterback, *Mekilta,* 3 vols. (Philadelphia: Jewish Publication Society of America, 1933), 3:171.

Was it the witness of the Corinthians' sins by Paul and his friends? There had been at least three witnesses (Paul, Titus, the brother, possibly Timothy, and many others), and there would soon have been three visits. Three witnesses had seen the persistent crimes three different times. The evidence of the Corinthians' sins was undeniable.

Beyond the literary and conceptual links, Paul's point in 13:1 could have been impending judgment of proved sin. In this view, Paul warned that he would deal in a legal manner with all remaining offenses. The quotation presents a proverbial rule for dealing with sin. The emphasis of this section may have been on the judgment that Paul would bring, apart from specific witnessing and an actual courtroom-like scene. This judgment would be exercised as in 1 Corinthians 5—by the gathered community. The quotation, therefore, is related to the finality of Paul's third visit.

Nevertheless, the fact needing confirmation (13:1) was not the sinfulness of the Corinthians, but the "proof" of Christ within Paul (13:3). Paul indeed mentioned not sparing anyone (13:2), but he set this statement within the context of the "proof" of the Christ who spoke within him (13:3). In this light, the witness was the Corinthians congregation; what they witnessed was the authority of Christ within Paul. When Paul was present during his second visit, he warned that, though he would leave with the situation still out of hand, if he returned he would bring the problems to an end (13:2). He had repeated this warning in 1 Corinthians 4:21 and did so again here. Those who had sinned in the past (13:2) were those referred to in 12:21, and "to all the rest as well" were any newcomers to the side of the opposition, either by overt participation or by the traits mentioned in 12:20.

Paul had warned the Corinthians of a coming time when he would give them all the proof they needed of the power of Christ within, but he had refrained from showing this severe aspect of Christ's power for as long as possible. The Corinthians would receive all the proof they needed of the Christ who spoke within Paul (13:3). Discipline for the Corinthians' sins was hardly mentioned in this chapter, compared with the emphasis on establishing the truth of whether or not it was Christ who spoke within Paul. Thus the "fact" (13:1) needing to be confirmed by two or three witnesses was Paul's apostolic credentials, the very problem throughout the letter. The Corinthians amounted to more than three witnesses of Paul's authority and would soon have witnessed this three times.

The Corinthians' desire for the proof of Christ within Paul (13:3) was like that of a child who refuses to believe his father has parental authority unless the dad administers a hard spanking. The dad will, no doubt, try to convince the errant child that the dad's love and authority is best experienced in less severe ways. But an end will come, and the father will have to use severity, lest the child grow more rebellious and distrustful of its parent. This attitude is wrapped up in the word "since" (13:3). Why would Paul spare no one? Because the Corinthians were looking for that kind of testimony. They had been used to rough treatment (11:20-21) and demanded it from Paul. He would deliver it, even though he feared such actions (12:20-21). Paul was full of care, even for the stubborn minority; they were still his beloved children.

"Who is not weak toward you" (13:3) reflects the Corinthians' confusion of the weakness of the apostle with the strength of Christ. Paul's weakness did not mean that Christ was not in him. The false apostles asserted that their strength showed their spirituality. Paul said that though he was weak, when it came to severe authority, Christ was not weak toward them. The meekness and gentleness of Christ is the context of chapters 10-13 (10:1). The Corinthians would not settle for that kind of Christ (see "another Jesus," 11:4), but wanted a Christ of status and power. Paul tells them they would witness such a Christ who would be "mighty in you" (13:3).

Explanations (13:4). The proof of 13:3 is elaborated on in 13:4-6. The Jesus preached by the false apostles had no part in weakness. The Jesus preached by Paul lived and died in weakness, but lived again "because of the power of God" (13:4). Paul says that here because the Corinthians could not understand the combination of weakness and strength; they were only comfortable with strength. Paul presents a mixed picture because Christ did also. Weakness caused His crucifixion. On the cross He appeared weak and subject to all the trials and troubles of the world, but through that weakness God redeemed humanity (1 Cor. 1:21-24). Christ's weakness is now replaced by a life in the power of God. Paul now moves on to compare Christ with Christians.

"We also are weak in Him" shows that believers, while on earth, share in Christ's past earthly weakness and thus participate in "the sufferings of Christ" (1:5). But the Christian's weakness will cease, as did Christ's, "because of the power of God." The power of God is in the living Christ, not in the outward appearance of believers. Their appearance is one of weakness, which masks the internal glory of the living and powerful Christ. This point was also made earlier in 4:7.

Warning (13:5-6). In that light, the Corinthians had better test themselves (13:5) to see if Christ dwelt within them. In spite of their grand claims, they could not escape the very weaknesses that they despised (1 Cor. 1:26). After all, among them were few who were well-born, rich, or strong (1 Cor. 1:26-27). If weakness disqualifies, could they themselves escape? In 13:7-10 Paul would back away from threatening discipline and once again stress his preference for showing his weakness rather than severe authority. To avoid such severity Paul asked them to examine themselves and realize that Christ dwelt both in them and in him.

Paul assumed that the Corinthians would certainly confirm that Christ was in them (13:5), but on what basis? They would have to view themselves as weak (13:4) or ultimately disassociate themselves from sharing in the weakness of Christ Himself. Paul hoped this examination would bring about a reversal of their worldly associations, a repentance from their past sins, and an end to their support of Satan's messengers. As a result of their witness of the indwelling Christ, Paul trusted that the Corinthians would realize that he and his friends also manifested Christ (13:6).

Explanation (13:7-10). Paul relayed yet another proof of his interests for the Corinthians, not for his own approval (13:7). Even if a minority of the Corinthians might not have been convinced that their examination confirmed Paul's authority, he prayed that the majority would do what was right. "Even though we should appear unapproved" emphasized appearance, not fact. Paul was approved before God, but not necessarily before the Corinthians. Even if, in the end, Paul and his friends did not gain human approval, he prayed that the Corinthians would do what was right regarding putting a stop to the sway of the false apostles and the long-standing immorality in Corinth. This further emphasized that Paul did not want to gain approval even through severe discipline. If Paul did not have a chance to be severe, but simply continued to be thought of as one weak in speech and appearance, then all he could ask for would be that the Corinthians do right (13:8).

"For we can do nothing against the truth" (13:8) explains this idea further. There was no self-serving interest motivating Paul, only the truth for the Corinthians. As long as they did what was morally correct, it did not matter whether Paul was given any credit. Paul neither rode on the glory of his people's successes, nor was jealous when they succeeded on their own or through the work of another. He worked only for truth, not for self.

If Paul was weak it did not matter, as long as the Corinthians were strong (13:9). The strength he desired for them was, of course, the power of Christ manifested through weak vessels. This is "completion" (13:9), the word (used in its noun form only here in the New Testament) that describes the result of God's will done in life—specifically, the correction of worldly associations that cause a warped opinion of weakness and an overestimation of status.

Paul reminded them once again that his authority was for building up, not for tearing down (13:10; see 10:8). Why this reminder? Because the Corinthians saw authority only as a self-exalting tool for power. Paul repeatedly informed them that true apostolic power was for edification. This also explains why severity in discipline was always the last measure, and in Paul's case something he approached with fear and much sorrow. Because upbuilding was Paul's continual goal, he was never interested in rushing into discipline, but tried several other measures first: staying away, sending associates, and ministering through letters. This entire letter was designed to answer Paul's prayer for their completion, which he hoped would occur before his arrival (13:10).

FINAL GOOD WISHES (13:11-14)

Closing greetings (13:11-13). Paul brings his letter to a close with a series of brief exhortations, summing up the thrust of the letter and its implications for obedience. The Corinthians were forever his "brethren" (13:11), never cut off from his love. "Rejoice" is more appropriate than "farewell," a possible translation. Paul uses the Greek word for "rejoice" throughout the letter (2:3; 6:10; 7:7, 9, 13, 16; 13:9, 11). Note especially 7:16: "I rejoice that in everything I have confidence in you"; and 13:9: "For we rejoice when we ourselves are weak but you are strong." An exhortation to rejoice, to be full of the correction and comfort of the Spirit, is very appropriate to this context.

"Put yourselves in order" (NASB, margin) is preferable to "be made complete." These closing exhortations are best seen as directives that the Corinthians themselves needed to put into action. "Be comforted" should be translated "be exhorted."[6] The idea is active community effort to mend broken fences by taking Paul's exhortations to heart, par-

---

6. R. C. H. Lenski, *Second Epistle to the Corinthians* (Minneapolis: Augsburg, 1937), p. 1338; Hughes, pp. 486-87.

ticularly his central exhortation to separate from worldliness (6:14—7:1).

To be "like-minded" (13:11) would have been to overcome all of the factions of thought and preference that were causing so much trouble. In effect, this would have excluded the false apostles from the community. Such unity would have issued in peace. But to "live in peace" is not an automatic goal. Whenever any might have found themselves tempted to engage in the fights mentioned in 12:20, they were to aim for peace instead. This had been Paul's strategy throughout his ministry.

This is the only place in the New Testament where we read "the God of love." Here love and peace are closely aligned. In this letter Paul speaks of his love for the readers (2:4; 6:6), the readers' love for others (2:8; 8:7-8, 24), and the love of God in Christ (5:14; 13:1, 14). Behind all is the God of love and peace, the eternal source of all that makes for peace in creation, among humans, and with Himself.

This letter displays love and peace of God: the God of all comfort (1:3); the Giver of the Spirit (1:22); the One who manifests the gospel (4:6); the Reconciler of the world (5:19); the Father (6:18). His presence guards against strife and provides the ability for obedience and joy. The stress is on the presence of God Himself, rather than on His characteristics or effects. The Corinthians tested the presence of Christ in Paul (13:3). The presence of God in Paul and, it was to be hoped, in the Corinthians was proved by love and peace; all else was from evil.

Some apply the greeting, "with a holy kiss" (13:12), to whenever Christians meet for worship.[7] The kiss, however, best refers to the specific problems at hand, community reconciliation for love and peace. The hearers of the letter were to turn to one another and express their desire for reconciliation by the external act of the kiss.[8] Such displays were

---

7. For example, R. V. G. Tasker, *The Second Epistle of Paul to the Corinthians* (Grand Rapids: Eerdmans, 1958), p. 191.
8. Lenski, pp. 784-85; Hughes, p. 488; Barrett, p. 343.

common in the Middle East then and now, and, like the Western handshake, symbolize trust and goodwill. The kiss had particular application to the closing exhortations to harmony. Though distant, the churches of Macedonia sent their greetings (13:13). That supported their goodwill toward the Corinthians and the mutuality about which Paul spoke in chapters 1, 8, and 9.

BENEDICTION (13:14)

The closing salutation is the longest of all the Pauline benedictions (see, for example, Rom. 16:20; 1 Cor. 16:23; Gal. 6:18; Eph. 6:24; Phil. 4:23; Col. 4:18). "The grace of the Lord Jesus Christ" was described in 8:9. His grace incorporates all the benefits and responsibilities bestowed upon one who receives Him. The presence of the grace of the Lord would keep the Corinthians always centered on applying His great gift of redemption, rather than on focusing on their own self-exaltation. If "Christ" embodies grace, the greatest gift ever given, then the "Father" is the source of that grace. "Love" is the willful and sacrificial act of God in Christ. His love is never separated from the context of His grace in Christ. In fact, as Paul labored to show throughout this epistle, love must be defined only by the pattern of the crucifixion and resurrection of Jesus Christ. Anything else will produce a different gospel and another Jesus (11:4).

All attempts at achieving unity and reconciliation in Corinth would be futile if they did not result from the "fellowship of the Holy Spirit" (13:14). The completion for which Paul prayed (13:9) had to be produced by the Spirit, who is the present pledge for future heavenly fellowship (1:21-22; 5:5), and the Lord in the church, who alone is able to transform it from glory to glory (3:18). He alone shines the light of the gospel glory on the darkness of unbelief and on the deception dwelling in a worldly Christian. The grace of the Lord forms the context and definition of the love of God. The Spirit is the potent presence of God, making real the promises of His grace.